THE ROMAN FORT
AND TOW.
OF LANCAS1

by
David Shotter and Andrew White

Centre for North-West Regional Studies
University of Lancaster
Occasional Paper No. 18

1990

ISBN 901-272-809

This volume is the eighteenth in a series of occasional papers in which contributions to the study of the North West are published by the Centre for North West Regional Studies in the University of Lancaster and are available from there. The general editor will be pleased to consider manuscripts of between 10,000 and 25,000 words on topics in the natural or social sciences and humanities which relate to the counties of Lancashire or Cumbria.

PREVIOUS TITLES
Windermere in the Nineteenth Century
Working Class Barrow and Lancaster 1890 to 1930
Handloom Weavers' Cottages in Central Lancashire
Flowering plants and Ferns of Cumbria
Early Lancaster Friends
Traditional Houses of the Fylde
Peter Newby: 18th Century Lancaster Recusant Poet
North-West Theses and Dissertations 1950–1978: A Bibliography
Lancaster: The Evolution of its Townscape to 1800
Richard Marsden and the Preston Charists, 1837–1848
The Grand Theatre, Lancaster: Two Centuries of Entertainment
Popular Leisure and the Music Hall: Nineteenth-Century Bolton
The Industrial Archaeology of the Lune Valley
Roman North West England
The Diary of William Fisher of Barrow, 1811 to 1859
Rural Life in S.W. Lancashire 1840–1914
Grand Fashionable Nights: Kendal Theatre 1575–1985

Printed in England by Pindar Graphics, Preston, Lancashire

CONTENTS

LIST OF PLATES

PREFACE

Lancaster is poised on the edge of a major new progamme of development, carrying with it the likelihood of new and significant archaeological opportunities. It is thus an appropriate time to review the existing evidence in order to present as complete as possible a picture of the fort and *vicus* at Lancaster, and their place in the surrounding rural environment; it is also important to identify those gaps in our knowledge to which attention needs to be paid in future research.

The recent publication of the reports of excavations over the last twenty years (Jones and Shotter 1988) has provided an opportunity for reappraisal with a good deal of new evidence now generally available. It is hoped that the discussions which follow will help to make that material more readily available to a wider audience.

We have a number of debts of gratitude to record: to Janet Atkins, Katrina Hunter and Patricia Kitchen for the preparation of the original manuscript; to Marie Ellis for help in assembling the material; to Geoffrey Harris for his photographs of inscriptions in Lancaster Museum (Plates 32–36 and 38); to Lancaster City Museum and Art Gallery for permission to utilize and publish a number of objects in the Museum's collection; to Peter Lee of the Lancaster University Archaeology Unit for preparing most of the plans and figures; and to the Trustees of the British Museum for their permission to publish the photograph of the Malpas Diploma (Plate 16).

D. C. A. S. and A. J. W.
January 1990

Study of the Roman settlement of the North West is of particular fascination. It offers sufficient evidence to make study and excavation worthwhile, but enough gaps and missing links to allow the luxury of speculation and mystery. We know, for example, that Lancaster contained a fort and settlement of significance. Evidence on its name and communication links with the rest of Roman Britain however, remain deliciously uncertain, allowing the least scholarly to speculate, unconstrained by hard facts.

David Shotter narrowed the scope for guesswork in his *Roman North-West England*, an earlier contribution to this series. In that he demonstrated a capacity to present the most recent archaeological research in a comprehensive and authoritative form, without making it forbidding to the wide audience in the North West that eagerly awaits work of this kind. In this study he collaborates with Andrew White to focus on *The Roman Fort and Town of Lancaster*. This provides a much needed survey of the extensive work that has taken place over the last twenty years, much associated with the energetic work of archaeologists based in the University. It also provides a firmer and more detailed starting point for the account of the evolution of Lancaster's townscape provided by Stephen Penney in another earlier volume in this series. The account is supported by detailed appendices listing Roman inscriptions and coins relating to the city.

In short, the authors offer an up-to-date account of an important Roman settlement, which will be of wide general interest. For local people it offers a particular benefit. It provides a basis on which to appreciate the significance of the next stage in the exploitation of the Lancaster's Roman archaeology, as the re-development of the city centre takes place. It therefore forms part of what remains an exciting phase of discovery, rather than simply a record of completed achievement.

Oliver M. Westall

LIST OF FIGURES

1

INTRODUCTION

Much has been written about Roman Lancaster. From the time of Leland, antiquaries have noted discoveries of Roman material and there have been several attempts to produce an overview of the present state of knowledge by writers such as Watkin (1883) and Leather (1972); both the present writers have been involved in similar works (Shotter 1973; 1984; White 1987; Jones and Shotter 1988.). Why then is it necessary to produce a further overview?

The answer is complex. Archaeological excavations, and the study of finds such as coins and pottery, allow us to make new judgements and to pose further questions. In particular the publication (Jones and Shotter, 1988) of many of the principal excavations of the early 1970s has produced a wealth of information on which both factual assessments and new theories can be based. There is a need, too, to translate some of the technicality of that volume for the benefit of a wider audience.

Some problems, however, remain intractable, particularly that of the Roman name for Lancaster. Informed guesses can, of course, be made, though the find of an appropriate inscription could radically change the position.

Recent archaeological work in the civilian settlement outside the fort has produced much new evidence for both the extent and layout of this predecessor of modern Lancaster, and there are hopes that further work will delineate the course of the river and locate the waterfront of Roman times.

For the first time, the fort itself begins to assume a definite location and dimensions, though the size of it presents some problems. Topographically an area between 10 and 12 acres would suit best, but this is exceptional for a Roman auxiliary fort. Possibly the site itself was exceptional; and there are a number of suggestions that could explain the situation. The earliest fort, of the late first century AD, begins to look more conventional and to have a different orientation to later ones. The final manifestation, as has been known for some time, was not only differently aligned, perhaps to protect a harbour, but was also different in scale and kind. The building of a new expensive type of fortification, more familiar along the Channel coasts of Britain and France, suggests an unusual significance in the treatment of Lancaster, which may go back to earlier origins.

In the surrounding countryside, intensive field survey and aerial photography have located some of the farmsteads which provided the food and clothing for the largely unproductive soldiery. Excavations in the Conder valley have revealed something, though by no means all, of a substantial industrial area based on Quernmore.

Finally the first overall study of the coin-finds from Lancaster provides us with evidence of a kind unobtainable from other sources, which also allows conclusions of a general nature to be drawn about the occupation of both fort and civil settlement.

We give original sources and first-hand factual information in full wherever possible, to allow this volume to act as a springboard to further work.

2

TOPOGRAPHY

The successive Roman forts of Lancaster crowned the prominent hill known as Castle Hill, where now stand the medieval Castle and Priory Church. The lower slopes provided a suitable site for the civilian population to build upon (Fig. 1).

Castle Hill is a natural knoll rising in two places to 125 feet immediately under the present Priory Church and Shire Hall. A larger area, bounded by the 100 foot contour, forms a fairly level area for a fort of up to approximately 10 acres (Plate 1). Beyond this the ground falls steeply away especially to the east and west. To the north a gentler slope once ran down to the river. This natural line is now somewhat disguised by a nineteenth century railway cutting and by the building of St. George's Quay in the 1750s. To the south, gardens of houses in Castle Park now drop sheer some 20 feet to Meeting House Lane. This is probably the result of post-medieval landscaping and originally the slope may have been somewhat gentler. Landscaping has undoubtedly affected the eastern side of the hill. Many of the gardens of the large houses in St Marygate (Upper Church Street) were terraced out of the hillside in the eighteenth century (Jones and Shotter 1988, 46).

The geology of the hill is complex, being composed of sandstone and Keuper Marl, with a varying thickness of Boulder clay mantle.

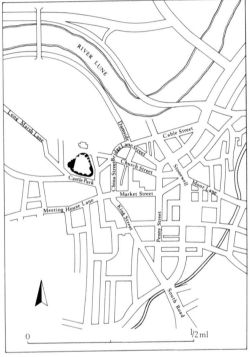

Fig. 1 Plan of Lancaster

Terracing and natural hill wash have affected the original contours but on the northern side the two large fields known as Vicarage Fields (from their former use as glebeland) have seen no substantial building activity since Roman times, and only limited disturbance prior to the 1927–9 excavations.

The earliest Roman forts took advantage of the natural contours and lay with their north–south axis along the ridge, with a relatively slight rise and fall, but a considerable change of level east to west.

Plate 1 Castle Hill: aerial photograph from the north-west

The fourth-century remodelling seems to have ignored these natural contours and aligned itself instead to the other principal natural feature of Lancaster, the river Lune, almost certainly because of the need to protect a fleet base and harbour installations. The Lune has changed its course since Roman times, both above and below Lancaster. Natural processes have been aided by the building of fish weirs at Skerton in the Middle Ages (Brownbill 1915, 184ff) and by scouring and training of the channel at Salt Ayre in the eighteenth century (Port Commission Records).

Originally it would appear that the Lune ran a good deal further south than it does at present, occupying a line now marked by Damside Street. By the Middle Ages this course had been abandoned in favour of another to the north of the island known as Green Ayre. The former line was taken over as a mill-leat to serve the Duchy of Lancaster's mill at the bottom of Calkeld Lane, and the mill-leat, now culverted, gave its name to Damside Street.

While the massive stone fort seems to have survived in part until at least the eleventh century it is curious that the more abiding topographical influence has been the layout of the earlier forts and the civilian settlement, much of which must have been levelled and demilitarized before the new fort could be built. Indeed, although the fourth-century defences are known only through part of their circuit, the evidence for their effect on property boundaries and the later landscape appear to be minimal.

The name of the Wery Wall recurs in documents from the eleventh to the eighteenth century as a boundary. We do not know if the name refers only to the existing fragment or perhaps to a more extensive stretch, or even to two sides of the fort.

The civilian settlement, discussed at greater length below, lay along two lines which have since become important topographical features in the townscape. The first is a sandy terrace rising from river level at Stonewell to 20 or 30 feet above that at the east gate of the fort. This became the line of a Roman road issuing from the fort, along which ribbon development took place. In the medieval period it became Church Street. The second feature, possibly marking another road line, is the modern Penny Street which with its continuation, Cheapside, meets Church Street almost at right angles. Part of the settlement lay along this north–south line. The present character of Penny Street is determined by the long narrow medieval burgage plots which its houses and shops still occupy. Underlying deposits exhibit varying depths of fine sand covering boulder clays. The sand itself ranges between white or brown and a distinct deep red at the southern extremity of Penny Street, and contrasts with the Boulder Clay which underlies the fort. Much of the *vicus* area has been cut by cellars of buildings from the Georgian period onward, presenting few large undisturbed areas for archaeological excavation to take place.

3

PREHISTORY

Prehistoric finds are rare in Lancaster and appear to be as randomly distributed as anywhere in the countryside. There is certainly no evidence for any concentration of population before Roman times, although it is hard to believe that the strategic importance of Castle Hill or the delights of Lune salmon passed unnoticed.

The prehistoric evidence is of little relevance to the Roman significance of Lancaster which was strategic and military. A Neolithic Mortlake type bowl, found disturbed by the foundation trench for a Roman building at 65 Church Street is the earliest object (Jones and Shotter 1988, 207). A palstave from Castle Hill and flint arrowheads from Clarence Street and West Road are the only other well-provenanced finds, except for an interesting group of Bronze Age urns. These were found from 1863 onwards on Lancaster Moor and its immediate environs and within the built-up area from 1840 onwards.

No doubt we are missing earlier records and some of the descriptions are not very explicit. There is indeed a strong possibility that some accounts confuse Roman burials with Bronze Age ones. For the sake of completeness, a list is attached of all known Bronze Age burials in Lancaster:

1. Penny Street 1840. One urn.
2. Queen's Square 1847. One urn.
3. Lancaster Moor 1863–5. Six urns, an accessory cup, bone pins, and a bronze razor.
4. Lancaster Moor 1872. One urn and accessory cup.
5. Bowerham Barracks 1877. Six urns and a polished limestone 'wrist-bracer'.
6. Alfred Street 1893. One urn and accessory cup.
7. Lancaster Cemetery 1894. One urn.
8. Penny Street bridge *c.* 1900. One urn.
9. Penny Street Corporation Arms (no date). One urn. (Penney 1975, 92: Harker 1878).

4

THE REDISCOVERY OF ROMAN LANCASTER

Lancaster has long been recognized as a town with Roman origins. Its name and its position on one of the main roads to the north put it on the itinerary of many famous visitors, including a number of antiquaries. Some of their descriptions are quoted below.

Two early misconceptions, fostered by antiquaries such as Leland and Camden, must be corrected. First, the view that the 'old town' had stood beyond – that is, east of – the Dominican Friary seems to have no basis in fact. This has been taken to mean that after the Scottish raid of 1322 the town was rebuilt on a new site, coincident with its Roman predecessor. In fact all the evidence from pre-fourteenth-century documents suggests that the main streets are where they have been since at least 1200. Camden seems to have fallen for a fancied resemblance of names to propose an altogether unhistoric 'Caer Werid', which he then established as the site of the Roman fort. The 'Caer Werid' notion has taken a long time to die.

Plate 2 The excavations of 1928 viewed by Mr. G. M. Bland, Borough Librarian and Curator.

In the twentieth century an era of scientific excavation began with a three-season investigation in 1927–9 of the Wery Wall and the Western Vicarage Field, led by Professor Percival Droop and Mr. Robert Newstead. If these excavations were less than conclusive they at least served to whet the appetite of Romanists for further work (Plate 2). The principal excavations, their directors, location of finds, and place of publication, are listed below for convenience. Excavations continue at the time of writing.

Antiquarian notices

a) In about 1535 John Leland the antiquary recorded (Toulmin Smith 1910): '. . . The old toune (as they say there) was almost al burnid and stood partely beyonde the Blak Freres. In thos partes in the feeldes and fundations hath ben found much Romayne Coyne'.

b) In Philemon Holland's English translation of *Britannia* (1610), William Camden states: ' . . . yet for proofe of Romane antiquity, they finde otherwhiles peeces of the Emperours coine, especially where the Friery stood: for there, they say, was the plot upon which the ancient City was planted, which the Scots . . . in . . . 1322 . . . set on fire and burnt. Since which time they have begunne to build nearer unto a greene hill by the river side, on which standeth the castle . . . And hard by it standeth upon the height of the hill, the onely Church they have . . . A little beneath which, by a faire bridge over Lone, in the descent and side of the hill where it is steepest, hangeth a peece of a most ancient wall of Romane work, seeming ready to reele; Wery wall they call it, after a later British name, as it should seeme, of this towne. For they called it Caer Werid, as one would say, The Green City, happely of that fresh greene hill. But I leave this to others . . . '

c) Leigh (1700) quotes the following in his 'Natural History of Lancashire' : 'At Lancaster, lately in digging up of a Cellar of Mr. Partington's, were found several Roman Disci and sympuvia, or Cups used in Sacrifice, and Coins, as some of Aelius, Adrianus, and Augustus Caesar; the Cups have upon their sides the Figures of various Creatures, and Julius Flavius in Letters; on the bottom of one of these appear'd very legibly these Letters, Regin.I. which we may easily interpret, a Discus used in Sacrifice to Juno, as she was stiled Regina Caeli. These and the foregoing Observations, together with the Roman Wall there, commonly call'd the Weary-Wall, abundantly demonstrate that ancient Town to have been a most eminent Roman Station at the least'.

d) William Stukeley came here in 1724. This is his impression of Lancaster (Stukeley 1776): 'Where the castle and church stand is a high and steep hill, length east and west; this was the Roman castrum. I found a great piece of the wall at the north-east, in the garden of Clement Townsend; and so to Mr. Harrison's summer-house, which stands upon it; it is made of the white stone of the country, and with very hard mortar, and still very thick though the facing on both sides is peeled off for the sake of the squared stone, which they used in building. A year or two ago a great parcel of it was destroyed with much labour. This reached quite to the bridge-lane and hung over the street at the head of the precipice in a dreadful manner: it went round the verge of the close north of the church, and took in the whole circuit of the hill. The ditch on the north side of it is now to be seen. I suppose it enclosed the whole top of the hill where the church and castle stand, which is steep on all sides, and half enclosed by the river Lune; so that it is an excellent guard to this part of the sea-coast, and commands a very great prospect both by sea and land. Here was this great convenience too in the situation; that on the south side of the castle walls, under the tower, is a spring. All the space of ground north of the church is full of foundations of stone buildings, Roman, I believe; and much stone has been taken up there. To the west of the church is part of a partition wall left of that time.'

e) Father Thomas West, who knew Lancaster well, gave the following description (1793): On the north side of the hill, below the church-yard, are some remains of the wall that encompassed the station. It retains part of the ancient name of the place, being called Wery-wall. Those who suppose it to be that part of the priory-enclosure-wall, which was situated on the north side of the church yard, may be satisfied if it is not so, by viewing the part of the inclosure-wall yet standing, which is a thin mouldering fabric; whereas the Wery-wall is a cemented mass, that nothing but great violence can injure. Another fragment of it stands at the Stile on the foot-path, under the west-end of the church-yard. (note 1793; this has been lately destroyed). It is frequently met with in the church-yard, and its direction is to the western side of the castle. The father of the late William Bradshaw, Esq. of Halton, remembered the Wery-wall projecting over Bridgelane, and pointing directly to the river. This could never be the direction of the priory-wall . . . At Bridge-lane this wall makes an angle, and runs along the brow of the hill, behind the houses, in a line to Church-street, which it crosses about Covell-cross. This is attested by the owners of the gardens, who have met with it in that direction, and always found blue-clay under the foundation stones. Though the station was one of the first which the Romans had in these parts, and, from its importance, the last they abandoned, yet, but few Roman-British remains have been discovered at it'.

f) Thomas Pennant, travelling to Scotland in 1772, saw this (1776): 'On the north side of the churchyard are the remains of an old wall, called the Wery wall . . . For my part, with Leland, I suspect it to have been part of the enclosure of the Priory.'

g) Christopher Clark's account (1807), part of the first proper history of Lancaster is also illuminating: 'The Roman wall, which anciently surrounded the station, was named Wery-wall . . . This wall may yet be traced in the Vicarage fields, the appearance of the ground there still proves that a double vallum once encircled the hill. A fragment of this wall is yet to be seen, adjoining the garden of John Ford, Esq. part of which, about eight feet above the ground and six feet in thickness, sustains the north wall of his summer-house, adjoining the Vicarage Field: from which specimen it appears to have been an exceedingly strong cemented mass, capable of withstanding the rudest shock.'

Many of the eighteenth-century discoveries from Roman Lancaster are now lost. It is fortunate that from 1835 the Literary, Scientific, and Natural History Society and later the Storey Institute managed to preserve other finds, though even from this period much information has been lost. There has been some survival between these and the collections of the City Museum (founded 1923) which has also at various times acquired material from private collectors of the nineteenth and twentieth centuries. Of these a number collected from building sites and road or sewer works, principally in Church Street, for example, Drs Harker and Howitt, Revs J. H. Hastings and W. J. Locke (of Halton and Caton respectively) and Peter Rogerson, a man with a chequered career, and who advertised his own Museum of Roman Antiquities in Bridge Lane in 1853. Others were Alice Johnson, who lived in Castle Park and collected much samian ware at the turn of the century, and B. P. Gregson whose garden at Caton long held the statuary group from Burrow Heights (Plate 3) and the milestone from the Artle Beck at Caton (Plate 4). Among the coin collectors were Corbyn Barrow, W. Jackson, B. Dockeray, and T. H. Dalzell (Plate 5).

A number of antiquities were brought together for the 'Old Lancaster Exhibition' staged at the Storey Institute in 1908 (Anon 1908).

Plate 3 The group of statuary from Burrow Heights (Photo: Geoffrey Harris)

Plate 5 Coins from the 1856 Bridge Lane Hoard (Lancaster Museum)

Plate 4 The Hadrianic Milestone from Artle Beck, Caton

Plate 6 The excavations of 1950, viewed by Professor Sir Ian Richmond

Plate 7 The excavations of 1971 (Photo: G. D. B. Jones)

Excavations 1927-88 (Plates 2, 6 and 7)

Vicarage Fields, 1927–9. Prof. J. P. Droop and R. Newstead.
  Finds in City Museum, acc. no. LM 29.16.
  (*LAAA* XV–XVII (1928, 1929, 1930). 33–40, 25–36, 57–72).

Priory Church, E. end, 1929. Prof. J. P. Droop and R. Newstead.
  Finds in City Museum, acc. no. LM 29.16.
  (*LAAA* XVII (1930), 71–2).

Vicarage Field, 1950. Prof. I. A. Richmond.
  Finds in City Museum, acc. no. LM 50.29.
  (*HSLC* CV (1954) 1–23).

Vicarage Field, 1958. Prof. I. A. Richmond.
  Finds in City Museum, acc. no. LM 58.25/1.
  (*JRS* XLIX (1959), 106–8).

Vicarage Field, 1965. Prof. I. A. Richmond. (Unpublished).

Old Vicarage, 1970. G. Leather.
  Finds in City Museum, acc. no. LM 72.9.
  (Jones & Shotter 1988, 19).

Vicarage Fields, 1970–2. G. Leather.
  Finds in City Museum, acc. no. LM 72.9, LM 74.87.
  (Jones & Shotter 1988, 38–41).

Vicarage Field, 1971. Prof. G. D. B. Jones and J. P. Wild.
  Finds in City Museum, acc. no. LM 72.9.
  (Jones & Shotter 1988, 26–30).

Mitre House site, Church Street, 1973. Prof. G. D. B. Jones.
  Finds in City Museum, acc. no. LM 75.2.
  (Jones & Shotter 1988, 46–60).

65 Church Street, 1973–4. A. J. White.
  Finds in site owner's possession.
  (Jones & Shotter 1988, 77–9).

Vicarage Field, 1973–5. G. Leather, R. Bellis, G. Shackleton.
  Finds in City Museum, acc. no. LM 73.64.
  (Jones & Shotter 1988, 61–71).

41 Church Street, 1973, 1980. A. J. White/S. Penney.
Finds in City Museum, acc. nos. LM 73.65 and LM 81.19.
(*CONTREBIS* II (1974), 2, 16 and IX (1981), 1–10).

1 Penny Street, 1975. A. J. White.
Finds in City Museum, acc. no. LM 75.34.
(*CONTREBIS* III (1975), 1, 30–33).

Old Vicarage, 1975. T. W. Potter.
Finds in City Museum, acc. no. LM 75.40.
(Jones & Shotter 1988, 31–7).

73 Church Street, 1978. R. Bellis & S. Penney.
Finds in City Museum, acc. no. LM 78.73.
(*CONTREBIS* VII (1979–80), 3–31).

47–49 China Street, 1979. S. Penney.
Finds in City Museum, acc. no. LM 79.22.
(*CONTREBIS* VIII (1986–7), 3–33).

10 Cheapside, 1983. W. G. Watson.
Finds in City Museum, acc. no. LM 86.65.
(*CONTREBIS* XIII (1986–7), 18–19).

80 Church Street, 1985. W. G.Watson
Finds in City Museum, acc. no. LM 86.64.
(*CONTREBIS* XIV (1988), 2–5).

Brewery site, Church Street, 1988. Dr J. H.Williams,
Finds in City Museum.
Summary in this volume.

The Roman name for Lancaster (Fig. 2)

Despite endless papers and discussions very few Roman sites in north-west England can be definitely associated with a known Roman place-name. Although many Roman place-names are listed in documents such as the *Antonine Itinerary*, the *Notitia Dignitatum*, and the *Ravenna Cosmography*, very few appear on Roman inscriptions and so permit correlations to be made (Shotter 1979; Rivet and Smith 1979).

In the north-west, we can regard as certain BREMETENNACUM (Ribchester – *RIB* 583) and DEVA (Chester – Eph. Ep. IX. 1274 a & b), as well as LUGUVALLIUM (Carlisle). It is likely also (Hassall 1976, 103ff) that cases can be made for MAGIS (or MAGLONE) as Old Carlisle and BANNA as Birdoswald. There is thus little hope of achieving certainty in place-name location, though the surviving evidence can contribute to a discussion of the probable names of Roman sites in the Lune Valley.

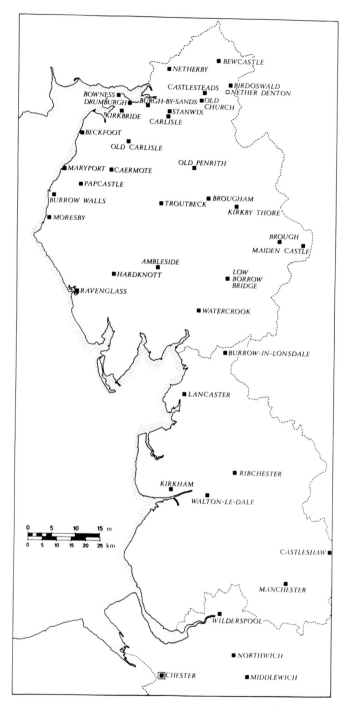

Fig. 2 Roman Sites in North-west England

13

Lancaster has not produced an inscription providing the place-name, and the Hadrianic milestone from Caton, although it states a distance which must run from Lancaster, does not preserve a name in any recognizable form. A unique piece of evidence, however, is provided by the dedication from Folly Farm (*RIB* 600) made by Julius Januarius to the God, Jalonus Contrebis. That this deity may be relevant to a discussion of the place-name is indicated by the discovery at Burrow-in-Lonsdale in 1739 of an altar (now lost) which was dedicated to 'The holy God, Contrebis' (*RIB* 610). It may be concluded from this that *Contrebis* or Jalonus Contrebis was a deity associated with the lower part of the Lune Valley. It seems likely that *Contrebis* refers to 'those who dwelt together' and has an apparent echo in Contrebia in the province of Hispania Tarraconensis.

Further, Jalonus is suggestive of at least one place-name which figures in *Iter* X of the *Antonine Itinerary* – Alone. The Antonine Itinerary is a document of the early third century, and its tenth *iter* describes a route of 150 miles which runs from Clanoventa to Mediolano, and passes through Galava, Alone, Galacum, Bremetonnaci (Ribchester), Coccio, Mamcunio and Condate. Whilst therefore Ribchester provides a 'pivot' for identifying the route, little else, north or south, is identified for certain. Many people, however, agree that south of Ribchester the route runs through Wigan (Coccio), Manchester (Mamcunio: Hind 1974), Northwich (Condate) to Whitchurch in Shropshire (Mediolano).

Northwards, however, from Ribchester, the problems are considerable, and exacerbated by the poor state of our knowledge of the occupation-chronologies of the majority of relevant sites. It would be important to know which sites were actually occupied at the time of compilation of the *Antonine Itinerary*; for it is unlikely that a site that had been abandoned (even if only temporarily) would find a place in the Itinerary's listing.

It is not intended here to rehearse the recent valuable arguments over the interpretation of distances in the *Itinera*, except to note the tendency of the Itinerary to fall slightly, but consistently, short of true distances (Rivet 1970: Rodwell 1975). It is clear, however, that scribal errors have in many cases rendered the transmitted distances far from sacrosanct.

From Bremetennacum (Ribchester), the Itinerary describes a stage of 27 miles to Galacum: two known routes ran northwards from Ribchester – one to Burrow-in-Lonsdale (31 Roman miles), the other to Lancaster (approximately 24/25 Roman miles, allowing for a route whose precise course is not known: Leather 1972). In this case, the Itinerary's *xxvii* could be changed to *xxiiii* with little difficulty.

From Galacum, there is a stage of 19 miles to Alone, and a further of 12 to Galava. Traditionally, Alone has been taken as Watercrook; whilst, however, the distance of 19 miles would appear to support this, it has to be said that, etymologically, Alone would appear to be inappropriately sited in the Kent valley, and that in any case the occupation of Watercrook in the first two decades of the third century is far from clear.

It might not be unreasonable to argue that the similarities present in the names Galava, Alone and Galacum have caused disturbances in the text, and that from Galacum (Lancaster) a 12-mile stage ran to Alone (Burrow-in-Lonsdale) followed by a stage of 19 miles to Galava (Low Borrow Bridge). In this case, these three place-names would all be located in the Lune Valley, which was protected by Jalonus.

The identification of Galava with Low Borrow Bridge occasions further problems: the route continues to and concludes at Clanoventa, traditionally taken as Ravenglass. It has normally been assumed that this identification is supported by the fact that the 'Clan-' element in the name, like that of *Glanni*banta in the *Notitia Dignitatum* indicates a 'shore'. Ravenglass might indeed be a market by the shore. Rivet, however, has suggested that 'Clan' means 'clear' rather than 'shore'; in this case it would not be unreasonable to place Clanoventa at either Ambleside or Brougham. In view of the fact that a road-route from Ambleside to Low Borrow Bridge is not known, it would be sounder to look to Brougham; in any case the position of this site at the junction of the major routes from Chester and York to Carlisle would appear to enhance its propriety as a market-place. The suggested scheme for the Northern Section of *Iter* X would thus be:

CLANOVENTA	Brougham
GALAVA	Low Borrow Bridge
ALONE	Burrow-in-Lonsdale
GALACUM	Lancaster
BREMETONNACI	Ribchester

The *Notitia Dignitatum* is a document which appears to give military dispositions throughout the Empire in the fourth century; its problems, however, are manifold, and it can at least be said that its information does not appear to be chronologically uniform. Northern England is covered in a section detailing the command of the *Dux Britanniarum*; this makes no mention of Galacum or Galava, but places *Cohors III Nerviorum* at Alione, which is presumably to be identified with Alone of *Iter* X. It can be said that, although garrison-sequences are imperfectly known at most north-western sites, our evidence suggests that there would be some difficulty in placing an infantry cohort at either Low Borrow Bridge or Lancaster, both of which have clear cavalry connections (Birley 1947). At least the absence of information on the garrisons at Burrow minimises that difficulty. It has, however, to be said that the failure of the *Notitia* to mention either Low Borrow Bridge or, more particularly, Lancaster is strange (Jarrett 1976, 16).

The difficulties of the Ravenna Cosmography are no less intractable (Richmond and Crawford 1949); a route, which starts apparently at Manchester (Mantio) and terminates at Kirkby Thore (Ravonia), includes Caluvio and Galluvio; these could be the Galacum and Galava of *Iter* X, although there is then no equivalent for Alone. There is in any case no insuperable objection to a route which follows the Lune, mentioning Lancaster (Caluvio = Galacum) and Low Borrow Bridge (Galluvio = Galava), and including also Watercrook (Medibogdo) and Ambleside (Cantiventi, which may not be identical with Clanoventa of *Iter* X).

The arguments can be endlessly rehearsed and mutated, because in the final analysis we lack the evidence from which to introduce certainty. It can, however, at least be said that none of the existing documentation precludes the suggestion that Galacum was the Roman name for Lancaster.

5

THE MILITARY OCCUPATION OF LANCASTER

The Roman fort-sites on Castle Hill saw many phases of activity, breaks in occupation, rebuildings and remodellings. Whilst the evidence of archaeology and of casual finds allows a broad interpretation of these phases, many details of topography and chronology of Lancaster's three centuries or more of military occupation remain obscure.

Topography

Many Roman forts commanded routes of communication – roads and river valleys – and thus did not naturally seek out the higher ground. At Lancaster, however, a succession of military sites was constructed on the eminence of Castle Hill (Plate 8).

The propriety of this seems to stem partly from its proximity to and thus ability to command the lowest fording/bridging point of the river Lune, which was close to the present Carlisle (Railway) Bridge. Secondly, the river ran closer in Roman times to the hill than it now does – following more nearly the line of Damside Street and North Road. This, together with tidal variation and the higher west coast sea level in antiquity, will have made suitable lower ground harder to find (Jones 1979).

From the first to the early fourth centuries AD, the forts lay astride the summit of Castle Hill, keeping, as far as can be seen, the normal rectangular 'playing-card' shape rather than adopting, as was once thought, an irregular polygonal shape like that of Bewcastle, where the fort's ramparts were apparently governed by the contours of the hill on which it was set. In the fourth century, a new fort with external bastions, apparently of the 'Saxon-shore' type, was built; its site came further down the north and east slopes of the hill, possibly, as at Caer Gybi (Anglesey), stressing this fort's connection with a point of embarkation.

In recent years, a picture of the northern part of the early forts has begun to emerge, with the recognition of the fragments of the ramparts and ditches of different periods, north of a line demonstrated by the position of the East Gate at the top (western) end of Church Street. To the south of Church Street, there is still little information, and certainly no *evidence* as yet exists for the position(s) of the southern defences of these earlier forts.

Plate 8 Castle Hill: aerial photograph from the east
(Photo: G. D. B. Jones)

With regard to the remodelled fort of the fourth century, the Wery Wall would appear to be the core of a bastion at the north angle, and some elements of a north wall have been recognised. It would not be unreasonable to suppose that, in common with some Saxon-shore forts, the keep of the Norman Castle was protected by the still-standing Roman walls, and that the Castle may therefore have been built close to the south angle and the south and west walls of the defunct fort. Further, some large scale structures observed in 1974 under salvage conditions at the south end of the Mitre Yard may have related to this fort.

Not only therefore do large gaps exist in our knowledge of the rampart circuits of these forts, but we are almost entirely ignorant of their internal layouts and structures. Thus, much remains to be done in recovering even a reasonable picture of the Roman forts of Lancaster.

The Military situation and Roman Conquest

Lancaster was situated in the tribal territory of the Brigantes, who were described by Tacitus as 'the most populous' in all of Britain (*Agricola* 17, 2). The territory of this large tribe seems to have spread from the Humber and the Dee (in the south) to a line north of that to be occupied by Hadrian's Wall. They appear to have observed the overlordship of Queen Cartimandua, though the nature and extent of their territory strongly suggests that in practice there must have been many local hegemonies having under their individual control such small communities as appear to have existed somewhere in the Lancaster area in prehistoric times (Penney 1981, 9). The existence of such local hegemonies appears to be the implication of Tacitus' description of Agricola's conquest of the Brigantes in AD 79 (*Agricola* 20, 3).

From an early stage of the Roman conquest of Britain, Cartimandua's stance was apparently pro-Roman; indeed she needed Roman support to be able from her own base, perhaps in the Vale of York (Richmond 1954), to control this large tribe. In particular, the Roman alliance will have helped her to dominate those whose loyalty was principally to her husband, Venutius, described by Tacitus as second only to the great Caratacus as a British warlord. His centre of influence cannot be pinpointed, but if Cartimandua's was in the east, then it is tempting to see his as located in the north and west.

It is evident from Tacitus that the marriage was one of *political* convenience, and that Venutius was frequently troublesome and in no way disposed by it to accept a Roman domination. Further, there are signs that Roman troops needed before the Flavian period to intervene to prevent large-scale hostilities amongst the Brigantes. In particular, the discovery of certain pre-Neronian coins (see p. 71) at a number of places in the north-west, including Walton-le-Dale, Lancaster, Barrow and Carlisle, suggests that the fort at Chester may have been the base for amphibious troops to sail from the Dee and make landings of a *temporary* nature in the Ribble and Lune estuaries, and further north along the coast.

Such Roman tactics kept the general peace until the temptation of Rome's own civil war in AD 68–69 proved to be too much. Venutius finally broke with Cartimandua to head the anti-Roman cause, and from that time the Brigantes were regarded as hostile and requiring proper conquest (Tacitus, *Annals* XII. 40 and *Histories* III. 45; (Shotter 1984, 5f and 74).

Petilius Cerialis, governor of Britain from AD 71–74, was the first to deal comprehensively with the Brigantes; in rather vague language, Tacitus says that he embraced most of the tribal territory 'either in victory or in warfare'. The completion of the conquest, however, was the work of Tacitus' father-in-law, Cn. Julius Agricola; in one campaigning season (AD 79), he swept northwards from Chester and York to Carlisle and Corbridge. The speed of the conquest was due obviously in part to the previous successes of the governors Vettius Bolanus and Petilius Cerialis, and in part too to the generally divisive nature of Brigantian politics; without major leaders of the calibre of Cartimandua and Venutius, the local rulers could be 'picked off' one by one.

Tacitus does not provide any details of Agricola's route, other than his reconnoitring of estuaries and woods (*Agricola* 20, 2). However, the weight of archaeological evidence favours a land route from Chester to Carlisle, probably supported by amphibious landings in the major river estuaries. The importance to this conquest of the Lune–Eden 'corridor' leaves little doubt that Lancaster, if not already fortified, will have seen a Roman garrison at this stage.

The Agricolan Fort (Fig. 3)

Whilst it is likely that Agricola's governorship (AD 78–84) saw the establishment of the first permanent Roman fort at Lancaster, it is conceivable that it could have been under one of Agricola's two Flavian predecessors – Petilius Cerialis (AD 71–74) and Julius Frontinus (AD 74–78). However, a distinction between these possible dates of foundation would be hard to make on artefactual grounds, and would require the ability to date closely a series of superimposed structures. In these circumstances the present weight of evidence makes it safest to assume an Agricolan foundation.

A major problem in assessing the development of the military site at Lancaster is the piecemeal nature of much of the evidence. There have been a few large-scale excavations and a lot of small ones (see p. 11), with the result that structures and sequences have been recorded from various parts of Castle Hill, though these are not always easy to relate one to another.

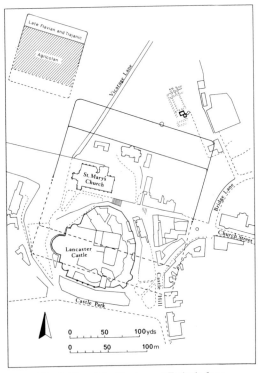

Fig. 3 Plan of the Flavian and Trajanic forts

Generally, Roman forts of Agricola's time were square or rectangular, with ramparts of clay or clay-and-turf (Plate 9). The external face of the rampart would be battered and the inside often revetted with upright timbers. Outside there would be one or more V-shaped ditches (and perhaps palisades also) whilst inside a metalled *intervallum* (or service) road would run all the way round the fort's perimeter. The buildings would be of timber construction, and the ramparts pierced usually by four timber gate and guard-tower complexes (Jones M., 1975).

Elements of such structures have now been recorded in at least four excavations (Jones and Shotter 1988) – Western Vicarage Field (1971 and 1972), Mitre Yard, South End (1973), Vicarage

Plate 9 Section through the rampart of the Agricolan fort

Field (1973), Old Vicarage (1975). These have provided details of the defences on the west, east and north sides of the fort respectively, and suggest a two-phase turf-and-timber fort in the last quarter of the first century AD which may have been followed by a short period of abandonment.

These excavations show a primary clay-and-turf rampart running east-west a little to the north of the Old Vicarage; this rampart was 9 feet wide, and, despite great vertical compression of the turves, still stood 5 feet high. Its battered front face could be clearly made out. It was constructed on a brushwood foundation, apparently to facilitate drainage. It is clear that this same rampart was seen in a more spread form running north-south both in western Vicarage Field and at the southern end of the Mitre Yard. The interior face of this rampart may have been revetted, at least in part, with vertical timbers.

Inside the rampart was an *intervallum* road with a fine metalled surface founded on cobbles, and carefully constructed where (as towards its eastern end) it had to cope with steep gradients. On the western side, five successive surfaces were detected. On the northern side of the fort (Old Vicarage), there were the remains of two phases of timber buildings, possibly barracks, inside the *intervallum* road. These buildings had been destroyed by fire. At the southern end of the Mitre Yard, traces of rampart and *intervallum* road material were found together with large post-pits which were evidently features of a guard-tower built into the rampart, and part of the eastern gateway. There appear to have been two V-shaped ditches outside the rampart in this primary phase, and at the southern end of the Mitre Yard these were seen to curve inwards as if to accommodate the exit road of the fort. This exit-road existed as a massive build-up of metalling approximately following the line of Church Street and St Mary Gate (Plate 10).

Calculations as to the overall extent of this fort are hazardous: the northern rampart would appear to have been approximately 615 feet long, whilst the eastern rampart (from the north-east

Plate 10 Build-up of road-metalling outside the east gate of the fort

Plate 11 Foundation-slots for timber buildings cut into the Agricolan rampart

corner to the eastern gateway) was approximately 200 feet. Assuming that the fort was orientated east-west, and that the eastern gateway was situated half-way along the eastern (shorter) rampart, the full length of this eastern rampart would have been approximately 400 feet, thus putting the southern rampart beneath the Castle. The area of such a fort would have been approximately $5\frac{1}{2}$ acres.

Later in the Flavian period, perhaps as part of the consolidation process which saw new forts being built at sites such as Watercrook and Ambleside (Shotter 1984), the early fort at Lancaster apparently underwent some remodelling, which perhaps should be taken in conjunction with the second phase of 'barrack' detected at the Old Vicarage. The absence of a stone revetment added to the north face of the primary rampart, and the presence of some clay rampart material in the ditch section excavated in Vicarage Field suggests that this remodelling consisted of pushing the northern clay-and-turf rampart some 123 feet to the north. If this happened also on the southern side, it would have made the eastern rampart some 650 feet long, producing a nearly square fort, and bringing the southern rampart to lie under the southern flank of the Castle.

It is not inconceivable that such a remodelling could also have entailed reorientating the interior of the fort through 90 degrees, thus making the north the main gate. Logic attaches to this in that, if it coincided with the penetration of the Lake District, the road leading from the fort across the Lune towards Watercrook will obviously have gained a greater importance. The area of such a fort would have been about 10 acres – large by any standards and capable of accommodating a large, perhaps double, garrison, which would have required extensive barrack and stable accommodation.

Foundation slots for timber buildings cut into the top of the primary north rampart are presumably the remains of reworked barrack-blocks (Plate 11). Some fragments of such timber buildings were revealed in a timber-lined well excavated in 1973; this well, which had been inserted into the eastern defences of the fort and which appeared to have been back-filled late in the second century, was lined with a quantity of *reused* timber. The evidence of joinery provided by these timbers suggested that they had originally been used as foundation beams or floor/ceiling joists – presumably from buildings such as barracks (Hanson 1985). Such a remodelling will clearly have involved also some reworking of the outer defences on the northern side. We do not, of course, know whether any changes occurred on the southern side of the fort; however, if reorientation was combined with achieving the proportions of a cavalry fort as demonstrated at Chesters, then we should expect the southern rampart to have been pushed a little further to the south.

Following these two phases of turf-and-timber fort there appears to have been a period of abandonment – though probably only short. The evidence for this consists of a silty deposit detected overlying the burnt timber 'barrack', and, as noted below (p. 73), the coin-loss sample which shows an approximately equal number of Flavian and Trajanic coins indicates an occurrence which interrupted the use of Flavian coins. The most likely explanation would be a late-Flavian break in occupation; a context for this might be found to exist in the decision in the late first century to develop the Stanegate road as the northern frontier of the province (Jones 1982).

The Second-century Fort

The break in occupation which followed the Flavian forts appears itself to have been followed by reconstruction and reoccupation very early in the second century. A Trajanic building inscription (*RIB* 604; see p. 60) was found beneath the Priory Church, and dates to *c*. AD 102; this may provide evidence for the rebuilding of the whole fort or of a particular building within it (perhaps the *principia*). Further, the Trajanic coin-samples and large quantities of Trajanic pottery suggests that the fort must have been in use for most of the Trajanic period.

All of the excavations on the fort defences have indicated that the enlarged Flavian fort formed the basis for the reoccupation; a stone revetment nearly 6 feet thick was added to the outer face of the clay-and-turf rampart, and at least one large new ditch was located outside the rampart in the area of the eastern gate. The recovery from this area of a considerable number of roughly-hewn, sharpened stakes indicates the presence of a palisade, probably on the inner lip of this ditch.

Traces of the *intervallum* road have been located in the excavations, and usefully these include one at the north end of the Mitre Yard (1973) which showed the road turning from north to west and thus proved the location of the north-east corner of the enlarged fort, together with what may have been traces of internal buildings. Building traces of this phase were also located in the western Vicarage Fields. Tantalisingly, however, it is not possible to identify the purposes of any of these building fragments.

It is known that the earthworks clearly visible in western Vicarage Fields, though not themselves of Roman origin, overlie the extended Roman defence-system. None of the excavations has located the position of the fort's north gate: however, a ditch running almost north-south, located on the northern side of the northern Vicarage Field, could be a drainage ditch associated with a road running northwards from the fort. If so, then this would suggest that the north gate might be located some feet to the east of Vicarage Lane.

Beyond the likely Trajanic construction period for this fort, topography and chronology become more confusing, though it should be noted that the extensive robbing of the stone-revetment, observed in all excavations, should apparently be described to the Roman period itself – perhaps prior to the building of the Wery Wall fort. As shown elsewhere (on p. 73) the evidence of coin-loss suggests that this phase of occupation came to an end in the early Antonine period, presumably coinciding with the new advance into Scotland.

Later Second and Third Centuries

It is likely that the Antonine occupations of Scotland did not outlast the early 160s (Hartley 1972), and that troops will have reoccupied some forts in northern England. It is unclear how far Lancaster was associated with this reoccupation. All excavated fort areas share in a paucity of pottery which is obviously of later second- and third-century dates, though it should be remembered that considerable confusion still exists in the assessment of pottery of this period. This, together with our lack of knowledge of the details of the internal layout of the forts, hampers an interpretation of the occupation-pattern at the time. Further, some areas indicate by a considerable depth of silty deposits that some parts of the fort at least may have been unused over a long period. Also the courtyard building and others excavated in the Vicarage Field, to which a late second-century starting date would appear to be appropriate, would probably have interfered with known features of the previous defensive circuit.

On the other hand, Lancaster has yielded an impressive sample of Antonine period coins AD 138–192). Many of these have come from *vicus* locations, but some have been recorded from the summit of Castle Hill (see p. 77). It should be remembered that the large size of the earlier fort suggested the possible presence there of a double garrison. In the light of *vicus* and probably port

22

development at this time, it may have been necessary to station a smaller (that is, normal) garrison in a fort which was not in total use.

Again, coin-loss figures would appear to support the notion that any military reoccupation in the late Antonine period had terminated again by the end of the century. However, evidence shows that by the middle of the third century, a cavalry garrison (the *Ala Sebosiana*) was once again associated with Lancaster; the inscription (*RIB* 605; see p. 60) which records its presence in the 260s indicates that at that time substantial reconstruction was taking place on the dilapidated bath-house and *basilica*.

The bath-house is presumably that located outside the eastern defences of the fort, a building of substantial and impressive character. The *basilica* mentioned would, in the context of a cavalry unit, most likely be a *basilica equestris exercitatoria*, a drill hall forming part of the *principia* of cavalry forts. A literal interpretation of the inscription would argue that the reconstruction was preceded by a lengthy period of decay. The extent of this refurbishment in the area of the eastern defences is hard to ascertain because of the amount of damage done in the excavated area by the activities of cellar-diggers. However, there were signs outside the fort's east gate not only of a very heavy build-up of road-metalling, indicating a long period of use, but also of a well constructed branch road running northwards from it, alongside the bath-house, and on towards the presumed harbour.

It has been suggested that the large courtyard building located in the Vicarage Field may have been an official residence, perhaps belonging to an important official – possibly a *Centurio Regionarius*, or a *Beneficiarius Consularis*, such as Lucius Vibenius of *RIB* 602 (see p. 59). Some circumstantial weight is lent to this by the find of a broken tile-stamp reading] FEC (p. 65). A possible parallel to this would be legionary, and may suggest that such an officer and the troops at Lancaster had a wider, regional, significance.

As yet, however, no recovered elements of the *fort's* structures appear to relate to this period of activity, and it is assumed that conclusive evidence for the nature of occupation at this time awaits discovery in parts of the fort site as yet inaccessible to study.

The Fourth Century (Fig. 4)

If military activity in the later second and third centuries has proved structurally elusive, this is not the case for the fourth century; for this period saw the construction of a major new military site on a different alignment from earlier military structures and paying more attention by its siting to the north and east slopes of Castle Hill. The surviving fragment of this structure – a masonry stub in the northern Vicarage Field – has long been known as The Wery Wall (Plate 12); it was only as a result of the excavations of the early 1970s that its place in the Roman period was left beyond dispute. The extent and character of the structure can be surmised partly from the results of recent excavations and significantly from antiquarian reports (see pp. 6 ff.) It is clear that the surviving masonry represents the core of a polygonal external bastion, presumably situated at the northern angle of the structure. The wall, which was between 8 and 10 feet thick, ran in a south – westerly direction (Plate 13), and has been picked up in the Old Vicarage grounds (1972), and reported again at a point some 50 yards south-west of the Priory Church (West 1778, 18) and again running west of the Castle (as it was in 1778). These observed lines could form an angle near to 90 degrees in the Churchyard.

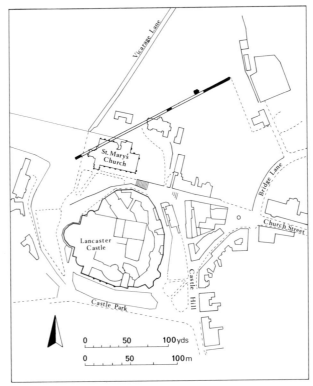

Fig. 4 Plan of the fourth-century fort

Plate 12 The Wery Wall bastion

24

Plate 13 The Wery Wall: masonry blocks of the lowest course

Plate 14 'Structure' at the south end of the Mitre Yard

Two observations relate to a not quite parallel southern wall of similar structure; West noted that this crossed Church Street, Covell Cross, and a structure possibly relating to it was located at the southern end of the Mitre Yard in 1973, though the circumstances of excavation gave little opportunity for the recovery of detailed information (Plate 14).

Overall, the structural fragments leave a great deal of uncertainty; elements of two walls – north and south – have been located, though they are clearly not quite parallel. The line of a west wall can be speculatively suggested, but is not certain. Far less certainty attaches to the north-eastern features; erosion of the northern slopes of Castle Hill may well have removed structures significant to this period, although it should be said that the hill-slope itself will have rendered construction of such a major structure hazardous. Indeed, it is not certain whether the structure had a fourth side; it could have been a three-sided enclosure protecting an embarkation point. In any case, if a fourth side did run from the surviving masonry stub it will have completed a four-sided fort of very irregular outline. Such irregularity is itself suggestive of Hen Waliau (Caernarfon) and Caer Gybi (Holyhead) and thus places these sites with Lancaster and Cardiff into a series parallel to the 'Saxon shore' forts of the south-east coast (Plate 15).

The northern sector of the fort was protected by at least one ditch; indeed, at the north angle the wall and ditch required the flattening of the bath-house which was part of the Courtyard Building in the Northern Vicarage Field. The surviving masonry of the Wery Wall, as stated above, is the core of a polygonal bastion: such bastions were a normal feature of Saxon-shore fort construction, and were used for mounting pieces of heavy defensive artillery, thus indicating the new phase of static defence to which Roman military philosophy had moved in the fourth century.

Plate 15 The bastioned fort at Caer Gybi

The overall size of such a fort is hard to compute, but may have been in the order of $5\frac{1}{2}$ acres, if the lines and extent of its walls are as suggested. There is no evidence concerning internal structures: indeed it is not inconceivable that the walls formed protection for buildings of a temporary nature used by both soldiers and civilians. The dating evidence associated with the Wery Wall suggests that it was constructed AD 330, and the abundance of fourth-century pottery and coins suggests a well-used site – for example on the Old Vicarage site, which will have formed part of the interior of the fort. The fact that Lancaster has produced significant amounts of late pottery and coins later than AD 378 indicates that usage of the Wery Wall fort extended at least into the earliest years of the fifth century.

Thus a tolerably clear picture emerges of Roman fort development between AD 80 and 150. For the next 150 years, severe problems are posed, largely because of the paucity of information from significant areas of Castle Hill. It seems that whilst artefactual evidence for military activity exists, we lack the archaeological evidence for contemporary structures. In the fourth century, some clarity again returns with the building of the Wery Wall fort, indicating a renewed military significance for Lancaster in the light of the sea-borne threats then current. Although much structural detail needs to be recovered, our surviving evidence suggests that this was a thriving period both in the fort area, and in the town that flourished east and north of it.

The Roman Garrisons at Lancaster

Although we possess fragments of information relating to army units associated in one way or another with Lancaster, we do not have sufficient evidence to permit a firm reconstruction of the garrison-pattern. A number of epigraphic sources (which are listed in Appendix I) indicate that from its foundation in the Flavian period to the close of the Roman occupation, Lancaster was associated with three units of the Roman army – the *Ala Gallorum Sebosiana*, an *Ala Augusta*, and a *Numerus Barcariorum*. The strong cavalry association received unexpected support from the large amount of horse-dung which was excavated from the well situated near the eastern defences of the fort (Wilson 1988).

1. Ala Gallorum Sebosiana

The bulk of the evidence for units of the Roman army at Lancaster concerns the Ala Sebosiana (or, as often, Sebussiana) – inscriptions on stone and tile, tile-stamps and a lead sealing. Only one of these, however – the Bath-house inscription (*RIB* 605) – is explicitly dated, and Birley (1936) has shown that it dates to a year between AD 262 and 266. It is therefore not clear how long was the Unit's period of duty at Lancaster, nor when it started or finished.

The Ala Sebosiana is mentioned by Tacitus (*Hist.* III.6) as part of the force which in AD 69 backed Aulus Vitellius' claim to the throne: Vitellius received support mainly from the armies stationed in the German military districts, but he was also actively supported by units in Britain. Indeed his eventual conqueror, the emperor Vespasian, found a confused situation in Britain, and sent Agricola as commander of *Legio* XX to deal with this. The Ala Sebosiana might thus have been part of the disaffected army in Britain at this time; alternatively, the presence at Mainz (on the Rhine) of a tombstone of one Marcus Sempronius, a *decurio* in the unit, might argue for a period of duty in the German districts up to AD 69. If this is so, then the reorganisation of the army following Vespasian's accession would provide a suitable context for its posting to Britain.

Early in the second century, the Ala Sebosiana is mentioned in two military diplomas – or documents of honourable discharge. These documents – one found at Malpas in Cheshire and referring to AD 103 (*CIL* XVI.48; Plate 16), the other at O-Szöny in the province of Pannonia (in Hungary) and referring to AD 122 (*CIL* XVI.69) – concern the discharge of soldiers from the British army serving under the governors Lucius Neratius Marcellus and Aulus Platorius Nepos respectively. The first quarter of the second century was a period that saw much military action in the north of Britain; whilst we cannot with any certainty place the Ala Sebosiana at Lancaster at this stage, it is worth remembering that a fort with a role of 'gateway to the Lakes' will have been of crucial importance.

We cannot definitely assign the Ala Sebosiana to Lancaster during the second century: whilst the dedication made by the cavalry officer, Julius Januarius (*RIB* 600) is generally given a second-century date, it does not specify the unit to which he belonged. Also, as we shall see, we have some evidence to believe that another cavalry unit, an Ala Augusta, has to be fitted into the garrison-sequence – probably at an early stage.

Numerically the bulk of evidence associating the Ala Scbosiana with Lancaster consists of the stamped and inscribed bricks and tiles found both at Quernmore and Lancaster (Jones and Shotter 1988, 143 and 186 ff). Most of the production of the Quernmore kilns appears to fall in the period AD 80–140, although a later phase of production cannot be ruled out.

The Ala Sebosiana figures on an altar found in 1747 on Bollihope Common in Co. Durham (*RIB* 1041); this altar was dedicated to Silvanus Invictus by Gaius Tetius Veturius Micianus, the prefect of the Unit, following a successful boar-hunt. The dedication is generally taken to be of third-century date, and could either imply a period of duty for the Unit at Binchester, or, more likely, suggest a visit made by Micianus to his colleague at Binchester (Richmond 1936, 113) – accompanied by the sort of conviviality we might expect of such a visit.

The lead sealing, found in 1973, reads ALS and IPD on its respective surfaces. Like the well-known sealings from Brough (Richmond 1936) where another ALS example was found, it was probably associated with stores or official correspondence.

In fact, the only dated inscription which refers to the Ala Sebosiana is the bath-house stone (*RIB* 605) which is now dated to the 260s. This inscription records substantial rebuilding of the Bath-house and Basilica in terms which might suggest either immediate repair work after an enemy attack or refurbishment after a period of abandonment. In the latter case, it might be appropriate to regard the Unit's presence as a new posting, although there is no reason why the Ala Sebosiana should not have been at Lancaster at an earlier period also.

There is no later evidence of the Ala Sebosiana, and it finds no mention in the *Notitia Dignitatum*.

2. Ala Augusta

The connection between Lancaster and an Ala Augusta depends upon the now virtually certain reading of the lost tombstone inscription of Lucius Julius Apollinaris (Edwards 1971), which was originally discovered in 1772. Although not dated, the wording of the inscription suggests that it might belong to the late first or early second centuries – but not later than AD 200.

The tombstone does not *prove* a period or garrison-duty at Lancaster for Apollinaris and his unit, although his youth (30 years) would suggest death on active service, which in itself would enhance the likelihood of Lancaster having been his base. Although no other evidence has been found associating Lancaster with a unit of this title, it must remain at least a possibility that an Ala Augusta was in garrison at Lancaster at some stage in the first or second centuries.

As noted above, Ala *Augusta* is a title rather than a name which will have been earned for meritorious or loyal service. Three Alae in Britain enjoyed the title – the Ala Petriana, the Ala Vocontiorum, and the Ala Gallorum Proculeiana. There would appear to be no time for the Ala Petriana to have served at Lancaster, since it is linked only with Corbridge (*RIB* 1172) and Stanwix on Hadrian's Wall.

The Ala Vocontiorum is recorded on an inscription from Newstead (Roxburghshire), to which Richmond assigned a date in the period AD 142 – 155 (*RIB* 2121; Richmond 1950, 21). This raises interesting possibilities, since the coin-evidence from Lancaster (Shotter 1979b) suggests that fort may have seen a temporary abandonment coinciding with the Antonine advance into Scotland.

The Ala Gallorum Proculeiana figures in four British diplomas of the second century (*CIL* XVI.69 of AD 122; 82 of AD 135; 88 of AD 138(?); 93 of AD 146). The latest of these diplomas was found at Chesters, which prompted Birley (1939, 213 f), to suggest that the unit may have been stationed for a time at that fort before being moved by AD 188 to Old Carlisle where it apparently remained throughout the third century. There is therefore nothing which would preclude a period of duty at Lancaster early in the second century.

Tempting, however, as such arguments may be, we have to allow that a single tombstone does not necessarily imply the Unit's presence at Lancaster in a garrison capacity at all.

3. Numerus Barcariorum (Shotter 1973)

The *Numeri*, *Cunei* and *Equites* (as opposed to the regular auxiliary *Cohortes* and *Alae*) were irregular formations recruited from the frontier areas from early in the second century to bring vigour and variety into the Roman army. Thus, after the Danube wars of Marcus Aurelius, some 5,500 Sarmatians were brought to Britain and split into cavalry units – one being based at Ribchester. The size of these irregular units was apparently variable, and up to the mid-third century at any rate they were often garrisoned alongside auxiliary units. However, the evidence of the *Notitia Dignitatum* suggests that in the fourth century they might often be left as the sole garrison of many forts.

Lancaster's association with a unit of this kind is deduced from the altar found in 1794 at Halton-on-Lune (*RIB* 601), recording a dedication made to Mars by a Numerus Barcariorum. It has been usual to identify this 'Unit of Boatmen' with the Numerus Barcariorum Tigrisiensium, which is placed in the *Notitia Dignitatum* (presumably late in the fourth century) at South Shields (Arbeia). If the identification is correct then it is likely that the unit was brought to Britain from the Tigris as a result of the eastern campaigns of Septimius Severus, and may have been at Lancaster during the third century before a move to the Tyne.

However, there is no pressing reason why the units should be identical, particularly since the *Notitia Dignitatum* records the existence in other parts of the Empire of *Numeri Barcariorum*. If the identification is not accepted, then we have greater freedom of disposition for the unit, which could have been at Lancaster at any time from the second century.

The *Barcarii* (or 'bargemen') were properly employed in ferrying and transportation, though there is no reason why their shallow-draughted vessels should not have been seen as particularly valuable for offensive, defensive or intelligence-gathering purposes in Morecambe Bay. In the third and fourth centuries the Roman army had to demonstrate increasing adaptability to cope with the new and growing threat of seaborne invaders. Such adaptability is vividly seen in the new Saxon shore forts of the south-east, in the signal-stations of the Yorkshire coast and in the use of camouflaged scout-ships (*Pictae*). Strikingly, the new fourth-century fort at Lancaster, of which the Wery Wall is a surviving part, itself demonstrates that the need for adaptability was recognised on the west coast as on the east.

Indeed, the new 'naval awareness' is demonstrated elsewhere on the west coast of Britain; structurally, fourth-century forts at Cardiff and at Caer Gybi (Anglesey) resemble the new military architecture demonstrated at Lancaster. The building at Lydney (on the Bristol Channel) in the mid-fourth century of a new temple dedicated to the Irish god, Nodons (or Nodens), is also significant; one of Nodon's 'interests' was the sea, and the temple contains a mosaic often taken to refer to the British fleet (*Classis Britannica*: Webster 1969, 158). It is possible that the two statuettes of Nodons (*RIB* 616 and 617) from Cockersands Moss have some connection with the Lydney temple and serve to emphasise the naval importance of the Lune Estuary.

Whilst it is possible that the statuettes and the Halton altar are dedications made in the wake of successful action by sailors based elsewhere, they also give us evidence for suggesting that at some stage Lancaster had a Numerus Barcariorum in garrison, reflecting the developing importance of Lancaster and the Lune estuary as a base for naval operations and supply. Indeed, following the example of other forts, we may suggest the possibility that for a time Lancaster was garrisoned jointly by an Ala and by a Numerus Barcariorum, when the site's dual role for land and sea operations was still maintained. In the fourth century, the Numerus Barcariorum may have been left alone in the new fort at Lancaster – its eyes now firmly fixed upon the sea. Coin-evidence suggests finally that this maritime role was maintained to the end of the fourth century – and perhaps into the fifth.

However, whilst a historical context in the fourth century would seem appropriate for this unit's service at Lancaster, two arguments point up a cautionary note: the high standard of lettering on the Halton inscription would appear more appropriate to the second or third centuries. Secondly, the apparent size of the fort in its enlarged phases from the late first century would seem to offer the best *structural* context into which to fit a large or double garrison.

Summary

In discussing the evidence for the three Units associated with Lancaster, we have seen that in each case very different conclusions can be drawn: ultimately this is due to the fact that only one piece of that evidence – the bath-house inscription (*RIB* 605) – is dated.

Although the presence of the Ala Sebosiana in Lancaster is fixed in the 260s by this inscription, there is no reason why the unit should not have been returning to the site after an interval of duty elsewhere. Indeed, since production at Quernmore is most likely to have preceded the Antonine period, the tile-stamps, which provide most of the evidence for this unit, would presumably be most reasonably assigned a date earlier than the 140s. Further, it should be remembered that the second century saw an increasing volume of the supply of pottery and tile deriving from large-scale manufacturers rather than from local kilns. At least some of the tile material from the fort's bath-house has been shown to have come from a source other than Quernmore (Shotter 1983).

Nevertheless, we cannot rule out a later phase of production at Quernmore, particularly since no stamped tiles have been located in any of the recent work on the early sites at Quernmore.

It is possible, therefore, that we should push the initial presence of the Ala Sebosiana at Lancaster back to *c.* AD 100. Thereafter, it probably departed and returned as the fort was abandoned and recommissioned, returning finally in the mid-third century AD. There is no evidence with which to determine its final removal from Lancaster.

If an Ala Augusta is to be fitted into the garrison-pattern, it would best precede the Ala Sebosiana; thus, a date between AD 80 and 100 would appear to offer the most likely possibility. Although a suitable context for Numerus Barcariorum at Lancaster would appear to be the new 'naval awareness' of the third and fourth centuries, the *nature* of the inscription which refers to it would argue for the possibility of an earlier date – perhaps sharing the large fort with the Ala Sebosiana in the first half of the second century. How long it stayed cannot be determined, though since the *Notitia Dignitatum* shows the importance of such units in the fourth century, there is no reason why this unit's duty at Lancaster should not have extended well into the fourth century, though perhaps punctuated by periods of service elsewhere.

Plate 16 The Malpas Diploma (*CIL* XVI.48: Photograph by permission of the Trustees of the British Museum)

6

THE CIVILIAN SETTLEMENT

Note: There has been much discussion in recent years as to what should properly be termed 'vicus'; the following pages employ the term for convenience to indicate a settlement outside a Roman fort (Olivier 1987a).

Location and extent (Fig. 5)

Outside the fort, from at least the early second century, a civilian settlement or *vicus* grew up dependent on the protection of the army and on its spending power. Here lived the wives and families of serving soldiers, shopkeepers, innkeepers, and others attending to off-duty needs of the army. There were also baths and temples, and official buildings where justice and government were administered.

It would appear that the settlement began as ribbon-development along the roads leading to the fort gates, in particular on the east side. Here, the line of Church Street has long been recognized as the main street of the *vicus*; its full extent has only recently begun to be realized. It is likely, however, that other gates also led on to elements of the *vicus*. On the west and south sides nothing structural is known, and the west gate may have been of lesser importance, leading out on to a marsh. The north gate, however, led to the river crossing and the road seems to have been flanked by strip buildings (Richmond 1959) as well as by a large courtyard building now best interpreted as a 'mansio' (or official inn), or alternatively as the home and offices of a regional official.

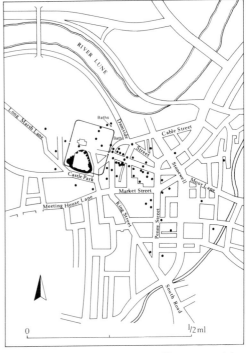

Fig. 5 Plan indicating find-spots of Roman material within the likely *vicus* area

It is not easy to determine the limits, because of the nature of the evidence. Scattered finds of Roman material in the Dalton Square and Quernmore Road areas may relate to farmsteads outside the *vicus* proper, or may represent material redeposited in more recent times. The best evidence for the limits of the *vicus* should consist of burials, since Roman law did not permit burial within a settlement. The cemeteries therefore tend to flank roads at the extremities. The slight evidence for burials, however, at present only allows us grounds for speculation (see below). The best guess is that the *vicus* covered the areas of the present Church Street, Cheapside, and part of Penny Street, together with adjacent parts of China Street, Bridge Lane, and New Street. So far no evidence has come from Market Street, which may well have been a late twelfth-century addition to the town plan. It is possible that the present Penny Street/Cheapside line perpetuates a Roman road, like Church Street, and that these elements of Lancaster's town plan go back a very long way indeed.

The foregoing is probably true of the *vicus* up to the early/mid fourth century AD, but there is no doubt that the building of a new fort on a radically different layout – (the fort of which the Wery Wall forms part) – must have had a profound effect upon the settlement. Indeed a large area of the former *vicus* must have been levelled to permit its building, and it is doubtful whether the parts not directly affected actually survived. It may be that the civilian population was moved within the new fort, but in the absence of any detail of its internal layout this must remain only a strong possibility, and in keeping with known fourth-century practice.

As we have seen earlier, it appears to be the early forts and *vicus* which have affected the present layout of Lancaster, and not the final Roman transformation.

Excavation and discovery

Finds of Roman material in the *vicus* area are recorded as far back as the sixteenth century, while Leigh mentions finds made in digging a cellar for Mr Partington in 1700 (Leigh 1700, 10), probably in the Church Street area (Docton 1957). The pace of discovery quickened as a major rebuilding of Lancaster took place in the eighteenth century, largely on the profits of the West Indies trade.

In 1772 the rebuilding of a house for Dr Wilson – now 80 Church Street – produced a great deal of evidence of occupation, including an inscribed pipe-clay figurine (see p. 61). The contemporary note on this discovery (Lort 1779) indicates that building work and consequent discovery was taking place on a number of sites in the same area. A very large stone found in digging a cellar one hundred yards east of this for a house for Henry Baynes was thought to be a foundation stone for a temple. Given the generally insubstantial nature of many *vicus* buildings this may not be too far-fetched.

These buildings are close to the east gate of the fort, but there is evidence for structures and finds further to the east, north and south. To the south finds are recorded along virtually the whole length of China Street (Johnson 1909) including the site of the YMCA, and the Black Bull Inn (now the Duke of Lancaster). Here, evidence included a red clay (tile?) floor at 8 feet below present street level. Later on, in 1936, a quantity of Roman material was found on the site of the Priory Hall.

The major sewerage excavations of 1853–4 produced finds mainly in the form of coins in the area of Union Square and Fleet Square and also at unspecified points on St George's Quay, all close to the river. The selectivity of Peter Rogerson, the collector into whose hands they fell, probably accounts for the lack of accompanying information. As the sewerage operations involved most of the main streets it is possible that other find-spots went unrecorded.

Further east the rebuilding of the Co-operative Society Store on the corner of Church Street and New Street produced disturbed deposits to a depth of 14 feet (Johnson 1907). Extensions to the south of this building in 1934 also produced several complete vessels.

Cheapside and Penny Street have also yielded finds. The tombstone of Apollinaris found on the west side of Pudding Lane (now Cheapside) in 1772 (West 1779) has long been regarded as evidence for an eastern cemetery marking the limits of the settlement, but it would appear that the stone had been re-used and excavations close to its findspot in 1983, though somewhat inconclusive, did not suggest either a cemetery or the end of the settlement (Ellis 1987).

The rebuilding of the Fleece Inn in Penny Street in the eighteenth century produced Roman finds, and others are known from areas to the south and west. The only certain burial (a cremation) was located near the southern end of Penny Street. The nineteenth-century literature gives some evidence for other burials in the area but it must be admitted that the descriptions are mostly too vague to be certain in distinguishing Roman from Bronze Age burials.

While the Penny Street cremation almost certainly marks the southerly extent of the *vicus* it is clear that no certain limits are yet known for the *vicus* to the east and north. The demolition of St Nicholas Street and building of the St Nicholas Centre in 1968, totally without archaeological investigation, may well have robbed us of important evidence in this matter.

Such finds are listed in the Gazetteer, but a number of excavations have revealed both positive and negative information about the civilian settlement. Probably the most significant building in the *vicus* was the fort bath-house; the existence of this was known from an inscription (*RIB* 605) found in 1812 near the junction of Church Street and Bridge Lane – that is, close to the eastern defences of the fort. Under salvage conditions, late in 1973, in almost this same spot (Jones and Shotter 1988, 72 ff.) substantial structures were revealed which clearly related to a bath-house. Whilst evidence was found of flues and ducting – in particular a striking type of hollow voussoir-tile (Shotter 1983) – the most significant discovery was a portion of the sub-floor area of a heated room; walls stood to a height of 6 feet, and floor-supports (*pilae*) in the form of tile-columns and rougher-hewn stone-columns were found. Still *in situ* were fragments of the *opus signinum* floor which these had supported (Plate 17).

Whilst dating-evidence was slight, it is tempting to relate the rougher stone floor-supports to the major repair work mentioned in *RIB* 605 as having been required in the 260s. The Mitre House office and car park complex has undoubtedly damaged this building, but it is likely that significant elements of it still survive beneath the new building, and may therefore be available for proper excavation in the future.

The first controlled excavation in the *vicus* took place in the cellar of 65 Church Street in 1973–4 (Jones and Shotter 1988, 77–9). Here building work to strengthen the ground floor involved building a column and disturbing the cellar floor, which revealed Roman pottery and cobbling. The subsequent excavation of an area 10 × 8 feet in the floor of the front cellar demonstrated a sequence of Roman buildings of which all levels subsequent to the mid-second century AD had been removed by the cutting of the cellar. The remains could be interpreted as those of a building with its gable end fronting on to the street (Church Street) with poorly constructed trench-built dwarf walls

Plate 17 The Bath-house outside the east defences of the fort (detail of floor-supports)

34

carrying vertical timbers 5 inches square. Further posts outside the wall had perhaps carried projecting eaves to shelter the timber-framed walls from the rain. The size of timbers suggested a single-storey building. Some windows were glazed, judging by the fragments of window glass, and the roof was tiled. Inside were several successive hearths associated with finely commuted animal bones representing the poorer cuts of meat. These had probably been cooked or turned into soup on the premises, or else represented the debris left behind after the better cuts had been sold (Plate 18).

This building had been burnt and rebuilt. A pit containing similar bones had been cut into the destruction deposit of the first building, so evidently the shop continued in the same business.

Plate 18 65 Church Street: Wall construction trench

The first building seems to have had a relatively brief life, occupying the second quarter of the second century. On the basis of this it could be suggested that the *vicus* was not established until the reign of Hadrian. There is some further confirmation of this, but more large-scale work is needed to allow this generalization to pass.

Further down at 41 Church Street (White 1974), the removal of the front wall of the cellar exposed debris and Roman road levels indicating a number of resurfacings. Burnt timber showed where a building had collapsed outwards into the roadway in the later second century. Such burning may not have had any sinister implications; indeed fires must have been frequent occurrences in a settlement of timber buildings where ovens and hearths were used. Further excavations took place at 41 Church Street in 1980 (Penney 1982), when the building was demolished and incorporated into the Co-operative Society Stores. Deposits survived in a small yard behind the former building, and hemmed in by three cellar walls, and from these could be identified two successive buildings constructed on vertical timber posts, in the second phase linked by a sleeper trench. The second building had been burnt probably in the third quarter of the second century, and the burning had preserved a mass of carbonized grain and carbonized wicker work. This suggested that the building had been a granary. Over the destruction a short-lived road had been constructed, running at right angles to Church Street and perhaps giving access to the rear.

In 1975 an opportunity arose to examine sections below present road level when 1 Penny Street was demolished and rebuilt (White 1975). The most significant discovery was a series of cobbled road surfaces representing a road running from north-west to south-west across the site. The earliest material recovered from the other sections dated from the later second century and the two together suggest a late second-century extension to the *vicus* flanking a road running away from Church Street and heading towards Great John Street or Dalton Square. The road also appeared to be heavily embanked. The section observed was over 10 feet wide, but was diagonal to the trench.

Three years later, in 1978, another site was examined at 73 Church Street (Bellis and Penney 1979–80). This too was a cellar, but this time a rear one, and set 30 feet south of the street line. Here a substantial ditch, running north-south and lined on its eastern side with posts probably for a boundary fence, had cut through a deep deposit of domestic rubbish. To the east of the fence were traces of a floor, itself covered with charcoal and mussel shells. The rubbish deposit dated from the end of the first century to the mid-second century, and the activity represented by the ditch and the floor was covered by a layer of heavily burnt clay and pottery dating up to c. AD 200. Nothing later survived.

Demolition and rebuilding work at 10 Cheapside in 1984 involved clearance of the frontage building, a yard behind, and further buildings, including the former Bull's Head Inn (Watson 1986–7). Both buildings had cellars, but it was anticipated that Roman levels would survive between them. In fact excavations were limited by the extreme difficulties of the site and the fact that subsoil levels were high, due apparently to a lowering of ground surface at some period. Indeed the only archaeological features, a pair of superimposed pits, were located on the extreme eastern side of the site. The lower pit contained pottery of the late first or early second century. The lack of features was disappointing, but the negative evidence for a cemetery here – (the tombstone of Apollinaris was found here or very close by in 1772) – suggests that the stone was reused and offers no proof of burial.

In 1985 limited excavations were carried out at 80 Church Street (Ellis 1987) in advance of landscaping work to the rear garden, which slopes northwards to the former river line. This house, built in 1772, produced some of the first recorded evidence for the *vicus*. The excavations were intended to assess the survival of Roman levels. Plentiful Roman material, probably thrown out by the eighteenth-century builders, was encountered, but no undoubtedly undisturbed Roman levels were located. The limited aims of the excavation precluded further search, but it would seem that the original report (Lort 1779) exaggerates the amount of destruction.

The largest excavation to take place in the *vicus*, or indeed anywhere in Lancaster, was carried out in 1988 on the site of the former Brewery between Church Street, Market Street, Anchor Lane and Cheapside. The results of this have not yet been fully analysed, but the following is a brief and provisional summary, by courtesy of Dr John Williams, who led the excavation:

'A good sequence of Roman occupation was found and the presence of Roman remains some 200 metres from the east gate of the early forts is in itself important, arguing as it does for a substantial settlement. The earliest structural remains, dating to the turn of the first century AD, comprise a section of a large timber building at least 18 metres long and a series of rather enigmatic parallel trenches about $6\frac{1}{2}$ metres long. They could have been used for holding uprights to support a raised floor, a system used in Roman timber granaries, but the trenches lack the regularity of plan associated with such structures. An alternative suggestion is that the trenches were for agricultural purposes but again this explanation does not quite fit the evidence. Hopefully further research will provide a solution. There was possibly a break in occupation before, perhaps in the third century, an alley-way was laid out over the earlier buildings and at right angles to Church Street. Timber structures probably stood on either side of the alley-way which was resurfaced twice but the site, on the basis of coin evidence, seems to have been abandoned in the middle of the fourth century, the very time when the 'Wery Wall' was being constructed. It is interesting to speculate whether there was any connection between the abandonment of at least part of the civil settlement and the erection of a new fort for coastal defence.'

Finds from this excavation were not numerous but two were of particular interest: a small fragment of wavy 'hair' possibly from a pipe-clay statuette and a beautiful gold ear-ring

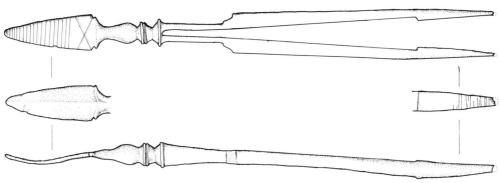
Fig. 6 A pair of surgeon's forceps (Lancaster Museum)

incorporating two ducks' heads in its design.

During the building of an extension to a wine bar at 9 Penny Street in 1987 (Ellis 1986–7) a foundation trench at the rear of the premises uncovered a cremation burial which had been in a pot, but which was spilled in the discovery. The lower part of the pot survived, a Black Burnished vessel not earlier than the mid-second century. Other fragments of pottery were found at the same time indicating further activity in the area. The finding of this, the first *in situ* Roman burial in Lancaster, leads on to a re-examination of earlier finds of burials. Burials were found on the site of the Corporation Arms in Penny Street in the early nineteenth century, St Thomas's Church in 1840, Queen's Square in 1847, and near Penny Street bridge, *c.* 1900 (See p. 5) Of these most are probably of Bronze Age date, but another complete Black Burnished pot, in the City Museum, seems to be the vessel found at St Thomas's Church in 1840; its complete state could be accounted for by its use as a cremation urn.

Apart from these excavations a number of casual finds have produced important information (Fig. 6); these are listed in the gazetteer. Two only need be selected for further comment; one of these is a tomb of tiles stamped ALSB (for *Ala Sebosiana*) found at an unrecorded provenance 'in a garden in this town on digging up the ground for new foundations' in 1752 or 1753 (Lukis 1883). Tile tombs are recorded from elsewhere in the country, particularly York and Lincoln. It is possible that the use of tiles bearing an official stamp indicates a military burial, and possibly one in a cemetery separate from the *vicus*. Perhaps it was outside one of the other gates of the fort, though on the evidence quoted it has to be in one of the built-up parts, which excludes the northern area.

The other intriguing find, again unprovenanced, is a set of four mortaria 'of progressive size' stamped DECANI/OFECIT (Johnson 1907). These it might be assumed were the stock-in-trade of a pot shop. However, the surviving example in the City Museum is clearly heavily worn and so the set is more likely to have belonged to a bakery or food shop (Plate 19).

So much for the eastern *vicus*. We now move to the evidence from the other sides of the fort. These can be dealt with fairly summarily, for lack of detailed information. First of all the area to the north, lying within the Vicarage Fields, needs to be examined.

In 1958 Professor Ian Richmond carried out excavations on the north side of Castle Hill, on Vicarage Field (Richmond 1959). He was under the impression that he was inside the Roman fort, and interpreted the evidence he found in that light. With the benefit of further knowledge this evidence can be reinterpreted. The principal discovery was a substantial third-century courtyard

Plate 19 Roman pottery from the *vicus* (Lancaster Museum)

building of stone, which overlay two earlier phases of timber buildings, belonging to the late second century. The purpose of this courtyard building will be discussed shortly (Plate 20).

Traces of several other buildings were found, one lying parallel to the courtyard building on its western side, and three or four others, interpreted by Richmond as barrack blocks, which appear in fact to have been strip-buildings in a northerly part of the *vicus*, possibly aligned to a road leading out of the north gate towards the river. These buildings, of which only fragmentary remains were located, were about 100 by 25 feet overall.

The courtyard building, a structure with an open court flanked by ranges of rooms on the east, north, and west sides, was found in 1973 to be part of a larger building whose well preserved southerly side contained a bath suite of several rooms. The whole had a long and complex history (Jones and Shotter 1988) and was finally demolished as part of the rebuilding and re-alignment of the fort in the fourth century. The courtyard building must have been levelled, its bath suite overbuilt by the Wery Wall and cut by the defensive ditch, but its underfloor part largely preserved by the upcast from the remodelling (Plates 21 and 22).

What the function of the courtyard building was is far from clear. It lay in the northern *vicus* area outside the walls of the fort. It has an official look about it, both in size and position, and could be a 'mansio' or official inn, used by officials travelling in the imperial service. Such a building has been recognized in the extensive excavated *vicus* at Chesterholm (Vindolanda). Alternatively this might have been the residence of some official of the region, whose status perhaps involved some show of affluence, or the entertainment of guests. Lucius Vibenius, the *Beneficiarius*, who dedicated an altar to Mars Cocidius (*RIB* 602), may have been such a person.

The remaining evidence for the northern *vicus* is interesting, if limited. In the Mayer Collection at Liverpool Museum are a number of artefacts found in 1849 when the railway link was made between the Green Ayre and Castle Stations. It is unclear exactly where they were found along this line but the railway skirts the foot of the hill and undoubtedly cut both the northern road from the fort and outlying buildings of the *vicus*. One group of finds is very tantalising, including as it does such items as 'offerings in the form of eyes, etc.' (Mayer 1852, 9). There is the strong suggestion here of a shrine, possibly a holy well, at which sufferers dedicated models of afflicted parts of their bodies in the expectation of a cure. Such items are known from elsewhere in the Roman world, for example, at Ponte di Nona not far from Rome.

Plate 20 Vicarage Field: The Bath-house

38

Plate 21 Vicarage Field: The Bath-house (detail of the *tepidarium*)

Plate 22 Vicarage Field: The Bath-house (detail of the *tepidarium*)

To the south virtually nothing is known. Even the position of the southern defences of the fort is not yet established, as excavations at 12 Castle Park (Penney 1977) failed to reveal any stratified deposits, as did excavations at the former George Fox School in 1989.

To the west the fort gates opened outward to the Marsh, an area much wetter at one time than it is now, and not likely to have been of much importance other than as a defence. A little to the south, however, at Westfield Village, off West Road, a number of burials were found in 1934–5 (Museum records). These were inhumations, and two were accompanied by iron rings; some Roman pottery was also found. Excavations close by in 1981 (Chandler 1982) failed to find any further burials or significant Roman material. The burials may form part of a western cemetery or alternatively belong to a small farmstead outside the *vicus* area proper.

In summary, the *vicus* seems to have occupied an area to the east of the fort roughly equivalent to the modern Church Street, Cheapside, and Penny Street, but running back a considerable distance from the present street frontages. To the south and west virtually nothing is known, but to the north another area of *vicus*, including an important courtyard building, lay between the fort and the river. Most of the buildings, on the slender evidence available, were of timber construction on dwarf stone walls, presenting gable ends to the street. Boundaries between properties were probably marked by drainage ditches and fences, recognized at 73 Church Street and on a different interpretation also perhaps lower down at 65 Church Street. Very limited evidence for burials suggests the southern boundary for the *vicus.* Other finds, from more outlying sites, may represent farmsteads. The many finds from the site of the Friary in Sulyard Street could indicate either a more substantial outlying building or, more likely, the collecting zeal of the medieval Friars.

Gazetteer of finds

ALDCLIFFE ROAD
1   Enamelled disc brooch found in 1979 (Museum records; *Contrebis* VIII (1980) 77).

ASHTON ROAD
1   Coin of Victorinus found in 1976, opposite Ripley St Thomas School (Museum records).

BRIDGE LANE
1   Hoard of c. 100 silver *denarii* found 15/8/1856 in digging for cottages (Watkin 1883, 188; *Contrebis* V (1977), 25).

2   Garden of 12 Albert Square, *c.* 30 coins found (no date: Museum records).

3   Bath-house remains and inscription (*RIB* 605) found 1812 in garden of Mr Willis at the corner with Church Street. Now on loan to City Museum (*Lancaster Gazette*, 14/3/1812).

4   Amphora fragments found in 1938. In City Museum, acc. no. (LM 258) LM 38.32 (Museum records).

5   Junction with Church Street, samian and coarse ware found in trenching road in 1973. In City Museum, acc. no. LM 73.16. (Museum records).

CASTLE

1   'Pieces of Roman Pottery' found before 1850 in Castle (Anon 1865).

2   Altar to Mars Cocidius (*RIB* 602) found in 1797 during alterations. On display in castle (Watkin 1883,170).

3   Handle of amphora? '. . . T.I.M' found in 1844. (Walkin 1883, 185).

4   Coin of Constantine found in 1980. In City Museum, acc. no. LM. 80.47/1. (Museum records; *Contrebis* VIII (1980), 77.

5   Coin of Valentinian I found in 1944. In City Museum, acc. no. LM 390. (Museum records).

6   Coin with chi-rho (Magnentius/Decentius) found before 1908. (Anon 1908, 56).

7   Coin of Nerva, found *c.* 1799. (Gregson 1869, 28)

8   Handle of amphora? stamped 'CAN . . . NCNI' found in 1819. (Watkin 1883, 185).

CASTLE HILL area

1   Brooch (dragonesque) found in garden of John Ford. (Museum records).

2   Flagons, samian, coin of Tetricus found before 1956. In City Museum, acc. no. LM 594/1–39. (Museum records).

3   Samian rim and spindle whorl from foundations of Storey Institute. In City Museum, acc. no. (LMA 262/2) LM 28.12/2. (Museum records).

4   Coin of Carausius found in Mr Willan's garden in 1860. (Museum records).

5   Pottery but no structural evidence found in 1977 in excavations at rear of 12 Castle Park. In City Museum, acc. no. LM 77.9. (Museum records). (NB. Alice Johnson lived at this house).

CASTLE STATION area

1   During building of station and rail link to Green Ayre station in 1849–50 Roman pottery, glass, and weaving comb found. Now in Liverpool Museum, ex Mayer Museum. (Museum records).

2   Marsh Lane junction 1849. Iron spearhead and Roman coins found. (Watkin 1883, 185).

3   Coins, one of Nerva, found 1965, in gardens off Long Marsh Lane/ West Road. (Museum records).

4   Coins found before 1908 at Marshrange. (Anon 1908, 42).

CHEAPSIDE

1   Tombstone of Apollinaris found in rebuilding old house in 1772 (*RIB* 606). (West 1793, 20; Watkin 1883,183–5; Edwards 1971, 23–5).

2   In cutting a drain, bones and pottery found in 1812. (*Lancaster Gazette*, 12/9/1812).

3   Pottery including amphora neck found on site of Reddrops store (7 Cheapside) in 1933. In City Museum, acc. no. (LM 50) LM 33.10)(Museum records).

CHINA STREET

1 During building of YMCA in 1908 rouletted carinated bowl found. In City Museum, acc. no. LMA 508. (Museum records).

2 Priory Hall. Pottery, metalwork and quern found during building in 1936. In City Museum, acc. nos. LM 185, LM 242, LM 36.31/1–47, LM 36.47.

3 Pottery bottle found 7 feet deep on site of YMCA in 1908. In City Museum, acc. no. LMA 509. (*Lancaster Guardian* 16/5/1908).

4 Coarse and samian ware found on site of A. Seward & Co. premises in 1908. (Johnson 1909, 111).

5 Coin of Faustina II found in 1973 outside Messrs Grubb's premises. (Museum records; *Contrebis* I (1973), 21).

6 Floor of a Roman building, tiles, coarse ware, samian, metal, glass, querns, coins (including Trajan and Antoninus Pius) found on site of the Black Bull, now the Duke of Lancaster, Inn in 1908. In City Museum, acc. no. LM 9.6. (Museum records; Johnson 1909, 111).

7 Coarse pottery and bones found at corner with Church Street, 1973, during GPO cable laying. In City Museum, acc. no. LM 73.16. (Museum records; *Contrebis* I (1973), 21).

CHURCH STREET

1 Large quantity of pottery including samian found in building Dr Wilson's house, later County Club (80 Church Street), in 1772, including pipe-clay statuette, *RIB* 608. (Lort 1779, 98; Edwards 1971, 25–7).

2 100 yards east of above on site of Henry Baynes' house, many coins and a huge stone believed to be foundation stone of a temple found in building work *c.* 1760–70. (Lort 1779, 98; Watkin 1883, 172).

3 Wall, coins and samian found in cutting drain, 1809. (*Lancaster Gazette* 7/10/1809).

4 Neck of large amphora found *c.* 1908 at junction with Bridge Lane. (*Lancaster Observer* 3/7/1908).

5 Trenches at corner of New Road revealed coins of Hadrian and Julia Domna and two querns. (*Lancaster Guardian* 22/8/1868).

6 Building work on new Masonic Hall site. Foundation trench, pillar base, and pottery. In City Museum, acc. no. LM 61.13. (Museum records; *Lancaster Guardian* 20/11/1959).

7 Samian sherd and tile from roadworks outside Sun Inn in 1979. In City Museum, acc. no. LM 80.14. (Museum records; *Contrebis* VII (1979–80, 43).

8 Amphora neck and handles found in 1925 at corner with New Street. (Museum records).

9 Co-op stores site. Various finds 1880–1901. In City Museum, acc. no. LM 11.4/1 etc. (Watkin 1883,188; *Lancaster Observer*, July 1908).

10 Samian base (Dr. 33) stamped DAGODVNVM found on site of Bank (now Natwest) in 1870. In City Museum. (Museum records; Watkin 1883,187).

11 Two coins of Trajan and quern found, opposite shop of Misses Brown & Wilson, 1854. (*Lancaster Gazette* 15/7/1854).

12 Coin of Constantine found in making a sawpit for Messrs. Nelson in 1854 (*Lancaster Gazette* 18/2/1854).

13 Coins of Vespasian and Trajan found in 1855. (*Lancaster Gazette* 21/4/1855) .

14 Five Roman rings found. (Museum records).

15 Rouletted beaker found *c.* 1850–80. In City Museum, acc. no. LMA 514. (Museum records).

16 Flagon found *c.* 1860. In City Museum, acc. no. LM 220. (Museum records).

17 Samian sherd. In City Museum, acc. no. LM 285/1. (Museum records).

18 Coin of Antoninus Pius/Marcus Aurelius found in 1854. (*Lancaster Gazette* 10/8/1854).

19 Square cap to column found at rear of no. 38. In City Museum, acc. no. LM 423. (Museum records).

20 Coin of Otho found December 1834 in garden of Jos. Dockray, St Marygate. (Simpson 1852, 120).

21 Samian sherd (Dr. 33) found 15/1/1930 at rear of 5–21 St Mary's Place. In City Museum, acc. no. (LMA 305) LM 30.24. (Museum records).

22 Samian ware, including stamp REGINIM, found before 1700 in digging a cellar for Mr Partington. (Leigh 1700, 10).

23 Pottery found in 1985 in service trench at rear of no. 39 (corner of Chancery Lane). In City Museum. (Museum records).

24 Coin of Faustina and pottery from trench between Co-op and Brewery site, 1983. In City Museum, acc. no. LM 83.37. (Museum records).

EDWARD STREET (north)
1 Coin of Faustina found in 1854. (*Lancaster Guardian* 31/7/1854).

FAIRFIELD ROAD
1 Rim sherd of samian flanged bowl found in 1982. In City Museum, acc. no. LM 82.59.2. (Museum records; *Contrebis* X (1982), 55).

FLEET SQUARE
1 Coin of Faustina found in 1853. (*Lancaster Guardian* 30/7/1853).

2 Coins of Domitian and Claudius found in 1853 in sewerage operations towards St George's Quay. (*Lancaster Guardian* 12/11/1853).

HILLSIDE

1 Coin of Valens found in 1984 in back garden of no. 4. (Museum records).

JAMES STREET

1 Uninscribed altar found during cellar extension at the Slip Inn in 1976. In City Museum, acc. no. LM 76.26. (Museum records; *Contrebis* IV (1976), 38).

KING STREET

1 Flagon found on site of Newall's warehouse, *c.* 1910? In City Museum, acc. no. (LM 368/2) LM.48.25. (Museum records).

MARKET STREET

1 Samian sherd (Dr. 37), style of Censor of Trier, found on site of new Co-op store 1957. In City Museum, acc. no. (LM 628) LM 57.4. (Museum records; *Lancaster Guardian* 8/3/1957).

2 Possible inscription found on site of Town Hall extension in 1874, destroyed by finders. (Watkin 1883, 184).

NELSON STREET

1 Coin of Victorinus found in 1966 in Storey's Car Park. (Museum records).

NEW STREET

1 Extension to Co-op stores in 1934. Pottery including two two-handled flagons found in building work. In City Museum, acc. no. LM 34.5 (Museum records; *Lancaster Guardian* 16/2/1934).

2 Flagon found before 1924. In City Museum, acc. no. (LM 27) LM 24.11. (Museum records).

NORTH ROAD

1 Handle of amphora, given to Lancashire & Cheshire Historic Society 6/12/1849. (In Birkenhead Museum. *HSLC* LXV (1913), 237).

PENNY STREET

1 St Thomas's Church. 'Cinerary urn' found 1840 during building of church; probably Black Burnished cooking pot; in City Museum, acc. no. LM 92 (*Lancaster Gazette* 21/11/1840; Watkin 1883, 185).

2 Cremation urn (Black Burnished cooking pot with cremation) and other Roman pottery found in 1987 in rebuilding work at Brambles Restaurant/Wine Bar. In City Museum, acc. no. LM 87.22. (*Contrebis* XIII (1986–7, 32–3).

3 Comer with Brock Street. Flagon found in 1850, in City Museum, acc. no . (LMA 172) LM 24. 18. (Museum records).

4 Samian sherds (Dr 37 and Dr 30) found at no. 10 *c.* 1930. In City Museum, acc. no. LMA 304. (Museum records).

5 Urn and ashes (Roman or Bronze Age) found in building cottage near Penny Street Bridge, *c.* 1900. (*LCAS* XXI (1903), 41).

6   Pottery including samian and millstone found 1764–78 in rebuilding Fleece Inn, Happold's Yard. (Cross Fleury, 1891, 454).

7   Pottery found in 1857 (*Lancaster Guardian* 25/5/1857).

PRIORY CHURCH

1   Pottery (including samian), glass, coin of Constantine found in building new porch in 1903. In Priory Church. (Museum records).

2   Pottery found *c*. 1951. In City Museum, acc. no. LM 449. (Museum records).

3   Inscription of Trajan (*RIB* 604), found during restoration of church in 1863. In City Museum, acc. no. LM 1892/9.

4   Many coins found in churchyard. (Watkin 1883, 188; Museum records).

5   Pottery, including samian, found in making open-air theatre in churchyard in 1973. In City Museum, acc no. LM 74.89. (Museum records).

QUERNMORE ROAD

1   Coin of Postumus found near Highfield in 1980. (Museum records; *Contrebis* VIII (1980), 77).

2   Coin of Domitian found at Highfield in 1981. (Museum records; *Contrebis* IX (1981), 36).

SCALE HALL, CLEVELEYS AVENUE

1   Coin of Valentininian II found in 1984 at no. 35. (Museum records).

ST GEORGE'S QUAY

1   Coin of Constantius found *c*. 1956. In City Museum. (Museum records).

2   Coin of Constantine found in 1972 near Pye's warehouse. (Museum records).

3   Samian fragment found in 1971 at Pye's warehouse. (Museum records).

4   Fragmentary inscription found in late nineteenth century rubbish dump, in New Quay Road. Probably derived from building work elsewhere in Lancaster. (*Contrebis* IV (1976), 22).

5   Denarius of Domitian found in rubbish tip in New Quay Road in 1982. (*Contrebis* X (1982), 56).

ST NICHOLAS STREET

1   Two skeletons and Roman pottery found in sewerage excavations in 1854 (*Lancaster Guardian* 8/4/1854).

2   Samian sherd found in May 1968 during building work on north side of multi-storey car park. (Museum records).

SPRINGFIELD PARK

1 Coin of Crispina found in 1950. In City Museum, acc. no. LM 435.5. (Museum records).

SULYARD STREET

1 Forty-two samian sherds and amphora handle found in digging in the Friargate in March 1821. In City Museum, acc. no. LM 315/5(1–42).

SUN STREET

1 Samian sherd from trench at side of Sun Inn in 1976. In City Museum, acc. no. LM 76. 50. (Museum records).

2 Samians herd from trench at rear of 67–71 Church Street (back of Sun Street). In City Museum. (Museum records).

UNION SQUARE

1 Coins of Marcus Aurelius and Antoninus Pius found 19/8/1854. (Council minutes).

OLD VICARAGE

1 Many coins found in 1830. (Watkin, 1883, 188; *HSLC* XXVIII (1875–76), 100).

2 Coarse ware and samian (including Dr. 29) found at Vicarage Tennis Courts, before 1909. Johnson, 1909, 111).

3 Pottery (including samian) and tile found in 1948 in garden. In City Museum, acc. no. LM 381 (Museum records).

VICARAGE FIELDS

1 Lead Seal ALS/IPD found in 1973. In City Museum, acc. no. LM 73.44/1. (Museum records; *Contrebis* 1, ii (1973), 25).

2 Roman altar (*RIB* 603 = *RIB* 607) found in 1811 or 1753 in garden wall adjoining Vicarage Field. In City Museum, acc. no. LM 73/1 . This appears to be one and the same altar, perhaps rediscovered in 1811.

3 The Wery Wall, last surviving fragment of the mid-fourth century fort wall and probably representing the core of a corner bastion. (Jones and Shotter 1988, 80–84).

WEST ROAD

1 Samian sherd marked 'Drususf' in cursive on mould, and boars' tusks and two coins of Faustina. (J. L. Whalley, annotated copy of Johnson 1907, 12).

WESTBOURNE ROAD

1 Coin of Valens found in April 1861 in digging foundations for 'Ashfield'. (Museum records).

UNKNOWN LOCALITIES

1 Tile tomb made of tiles stamped ALSB found in 1753 'in a garden in this town in digging up the ground for new foundations'. (Lukis 1883, 240–1) .

7

ROADS, INDUSTRY AND AGRICULTURE

The growth and development of the Roman fort and *vicus* brought dramatic changes to the landscape of Lancaster itself; it was also responsible for changes, physical and economic, in the hinterland of the Roman site, for its size, longevity and evident success will have encouraged developments further afield. The need for timber for building and burning will have brought some deforestation, no doubt freeing some land for agricultural use. However, in other ways too the local economy will have adapted to take advantage of the new opportunities offered by a Roman garrison and its attendant civilian population.

It is to be assumed that a certain area, now virtually impossible to define, came under the jurisdiction of the military commander at Lancaster. Some of this *territorium* would probably have been commandeered by the Roman authorities for their own use – land for growing grain for the garrison or for distribution as discharge-payments to retired soldiers; perhaps also woodland which might be used for its timber or even for hunting the red deer and wild boar which would have abounded there. Some land, particularly where suitable raw materials were available, was perhaps used for industrial purposes either by the army itself or by 'private' companies. Much, however, was left in the hands of local farmers, as owners or tenants. From them some produce was taken by way of taxation, but leaving more to provide for the farmer's family and to be sold on the open market.

The Vindolanda (Chesterholm) writing-tablets provide evidence for the variety of such produce; and we should assume that local farmers and manufacturers were sensitive to 'market forces'. Lancaster's hinterland will have provided the opportunity for arable farming, and for stock management at higher altitudes and in the more wooded areas. It is also worth keeping in mind the fact that Lancaster's position on a navigable estuary will have brought it importance as a staging-post for the transmission of goods further inland, and perhaps at considerable distances. This, too, will have provided opportunities for those locals enterprising enough to take advantage of them.

The Road System (Fig. 7)

Roman roads around Lancaster will have had their origins in military necessity, though it is obvious that they had a highly significant part to play in the broader development of the area. Not only were there the main routes, but undoubtedly a growing network of minor tracks which served to link farms and businesses with the main routes.

Milestones stood along the main routes, marking out miles which according to different methods of calculation, could be between 1600 yards and 1800 yards. The Lancaster area has produced three certain milestones (see p. 63): the fine cylindrical shaft of Hadrianic date, found in

47

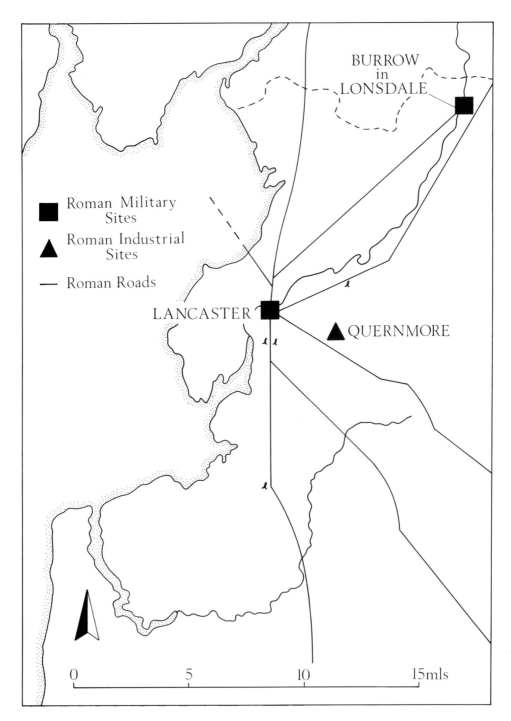

Fig. 7 Roman roads within a ten-mile radius of Lancaster

the Artle Beck at Caton, and two rougher specimens of Philip I and Trajan Decius, from the Burrow Heights area. In addition, a cylindrical stump in the gateway of Forton Hall may be a fragment of another (Edwards 1969,106; Plate 23). Given the size of these objects, it is unlikely that they will

Plate 23 Stump of cylindrical milestone near Forton Hall

in subsequent years have been moved far (if at all) from the spots where they stood. It is unlikely that these milestones are any help in defining Lancaster's *territorium*, as they would indicate an area smaller than Lancaster's significance would appear to demand.

The Roman roads around Lancaster have been much discussed over the years, and offer the usual wide scope for speculation. In recent years, much detailed information about them has been recorded by Geoffrey Leather (1972) and Robert Bellis (*Contrebis* I (1973) and II (1974); thus the present discussion will be limited to general observations on the evidence. The bulk of the evidence is derived from placenames, old records, scattered finds of Roman material, as well as from surviving features such as old roads and tracks (either in or out of present use). Such evidence provides many candidates for consideration as possible lines of Roman roads.

Further, this and any other area will have been crossed not just by major routes of communication, but also by many minor trackways branching from them and providing access to farms and other sites. It is worth, however, sounding a note of caution: whilst it may often be possible to designate a road as 'old', this does not necessarily mean that it can be assumed to be of Roman origin.

From the south, Lancaster was approached apparently by two roads – from Walton-le-Dale and from Ribchester (Plate 24) which probably converged near Galgate. North of Galgate and slightly to the west of the old road to Lancaster, there is some evidence of a raised line (*agger*) flanked in places by ditches. This leads in the direction of Burrow Heights, which is itself the site of rectangular earthwork. It was probably near here that two milestones and a group of statuary were found (Edwards 1971; on p. 63). The line continues over Ripley Heights, where at various times a metalled surface has been revealed by trenching. This line may have

Plate 24 Kerbstones of the Roman road from Ribchester to Lancaster, near Street (Photo: H. Sherdley)

followed Penny Street and Cheapside, with a branch leading to Castle Hill by way of High Street.

It has been argued (Jones 1968) that this route running up the west coast may have been formally laid out as a whole in the later years of the first century AD. At this time, it has been suggested (above on p. 21) that the fort on Castle Hill may have been reorientated so that its main functional axis became north/south. Previous to this the line south and, from Galgate, south-east to Ribchester was probably more significant, as well as the road out of the fort's east gate along Church Street. The road north crosses the river and leads directly to Foley Farm (the find-spot of *RIB* 600: see p. 58), and thus to Standerlands, Slyne and Bolton-le-Sands. A branch from this to Redbank Farm may indicate a road leading across the sands of Morecambe Bay, and aiming ultimately for Ravenglass, or another (as yet unknown) site in Furness. The north road gave access ultimately to Watercrook and the Lake District.

The road that led out of the fort's east gate was probably initially the most important of its exit routes. It followed along Church Street, and probably divided into two at Stonewell. One road led across the Ridge, by Moor Side and Old Hall Farm to Caton and Brookhouse. The Caton/ Brookhouse road crossed Artle Beck, where the Hadrianic milestone was found, and thence led to Hornby and Burrow-in-Lonsdale. The other road that branched at Stonewell led south-eastwards to Quernmore where some particularly straight alignments are to be seen. Such a road would appear to lead ultimately to Lincoln, which might imply that the road originated when the base of *Legio* IX was at Lincoln rather than York – that is, before the early 70s. This road runs close to the Quernmore tilery site at Low Pleasant.

Finally, it would appear that there was also a road from Lancaster on the *northern* bank of the Lune. This led through Halton and Arkholme towards a fording place just south of Whittington and thus gaining access to Burrow-in-Lonsdale.

The maintenance of these and other roads in the fort's *territorium* will have been the responsibility of the fort commander. Good maintenance and good security will have been the essential prerequisites for those with products to sell to the soldiers and *vicani* of Lancaster. In this way, the area's economy could develop.

Industry

Much industrial activity will have concentrated in the *vicus*, perhaps even organised into particular parts of it, as apparently happened at Manchester (Jones and Grealey 1974). Some raw material – clay, hides, iron-ore and so forth – no doubt came from the immediate area, but more will have been imported into Lancaster; for example, iron-ore from Furness. Lancaster may in addition have been an important centre for the movement of raw materials and finished products into and out of the area. Whilst users of Lancaster's port facilities will have been at the mercy of tides, it is likely that the *Barcarii* mentioned on *RIB* 601 (see p. 59) could have helped in unloading ships in deeper water. Alternatively, other (nearby) anchorages might be surmised, followed by land journeys. It is possible to envisage in this connection the use of Glasson Dock, or perhaps Thornbush further south and presumably close to the find-spot of the Nodons statuettes (see p. 62).

There must have been a good deal of small-scale local industrial activity in the Roman period, although much of the evidence is equivocal in one way or another. An iron-roasting hearth was partially excavated in 1972 at Quernmore (Low Pleasant; Plate 25). Its presence close to a lime-kiln suggests that, assuming that this activity is of Roman date, there may have been a larger

Plate 25 General view of the Low Pleasant site at Quernmore

assemblage of industrial activity in the area. Further, Warton Crag (near Carnforth) has produced evidence in the forms of a pair of scales and iron slag, which suggests metal-working somewhere in the vicinity, and certainly gives a strong probability of the extraction of the raw material for Iron-working from Warton Crag (Penney 1983). It would not be at all unreasonable to find some local farm-sites 'diversified' into such industrial activity. Indeed, the lead sealing of the *Ala Sebosiana* (see p. 65) might represent a fragmentary view of the despatching to other military sites of raw materials from the Lancaster area.

It is not likely that such activities will have been other than small-scale, and those involved in them will presumably have felt themselves under growing pressure, particularly during the second and early third centuries, from the larger and better organized sites which were winning large military contracts – for example, Wilderspool (Hinchcliffe and Williams f/c) and the large-scale pottery manufacture in central southern England and in the Nene Valley.

The largest bulk of evidence concerns the manufacture of tiles, bricks and pottery in the Quernmore area; two sites of such manufacture are known for certain: Lythe Brow and Low Pleasant. In both cases, recent work (Leather and Webster 1988) represents a 'rediscovery' of sites known at earlier times.

At Lythe Brow, there is a great deal of evidence in the form of debris resulting from pottery and brick making, although no kilns have been found intact. Although some of this debris is undoubtedly post-Roman in date, the Roman material appears to fall within the period *c.* AD 80–150, that is, approximately the first three phases of the fort at Lancaster (see p. 18). The first mention of sites, apparently in this area, was made by Father Thomas West in the eighteenth century. He reported the discovery of quantities of tiles and bricks bearing the stamp of the *Ala Sebosiana* (Leather and Webster 1988, 92 f; Watkin 1883, 175 ff; Fig. 9b). No examples of such stamped tiles have been recovered in the recent work, and it therefore remains open to question whether the sites which have been rediscovered are *precisely* those referred to by Father West. Thus, whilst the stamped tiles certainly suggest the presence of a tilery run by the Roman army itself, this does not preclude the presence also of private firms operating in the area. In any case, it is likely that such manufacture was widely spread across the Quernmore area in Roman times, and that further sites therefore await discovery.

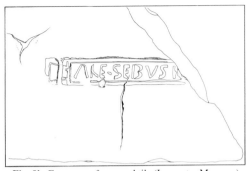
Fig. 9b Fragment of stamped tile (Lancaster Museum)

The Lythe Brow sites are situated close to the 300-foot contour line – perhaps the level of occurrence of suitable raw materials; approximately $4\frac{1}{2}$ miles to the south-west and on the same contour line further evidence of pottery and tile manufacture has been discovered at Low Pleasant, a site where iron-working has already been mentioned (see p. 50). Again, the excavation of two kilns in the 1970s represented the rediscovery of sites previously located – this time at the beginning of the twentieth century by Miss Alice Johnson.

The kilns were built into a low ridge with their fire tunnels facing west-north-west to take advantage of the prevailing wind. Here structural evidence was far more complete than at Lythe Brow; one had a subrectangular kiln floor and gave the impression of a construction that was sturdy, though lacking the precision usually associated with sites operated by the Roman army (Grimes 1930; Hogg 1965). It is likely that this kiln was concerned with the manufacture of bricks and tiles; again, no stamped tiles were found, which is also suggestive of a civilian operation. In the vicinity there was much debris of pottery-making, suggesting that further kilns await discovery. Two potters' stamps have been found on sherds clearly of local origin – one indicating a potter named TRITVS, the other an 'illiterate' stamp. These stamps, too, are suggestive of a civilian site (Plate 26).

Close to the tile-kiln was another which appears to have been used for lime-burning, probably itself connected with the nearby iron-roasting hearth. This, too, displayed substantial construction. Neither Low Pleasant nor Lythe Brow have so far produced any evidence of buildings that might be associated with their activities (Plate 27).

The pottery from the Low Pleasant site has predominantly been placed in the period *c.* 80–150, and suggests, as does Lythe Brow, manufacture which 'filled the gap' prior to the swamping of the market by the larger suppliers in other parts of the country. A good deal of 'Quernmore ware' has also been found in excavations at Lancaster and it may have reached other nearby Roman sites. The dating evidence currently available would suggest that the activities of Quernmore potters were substantially curtailed by the general Hadrianic reorganisation of pottery supplies, and by the

Plate 26 Low Pleasant, Quernmore: tile-kiln

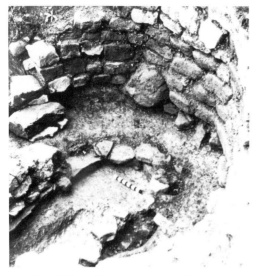

Plate 28 Pottery from the Quernmore kilns
(Lancaster Museum)

Plate 27 Low Pleasant, Quernmore: lime-kiln

less continuous military occupation at Lancaster evident from the mid-second century onwards. 'Quernmore ware' is of a distinctive soft pink fabric with sandy inclusions. Products include carinated and reeded-rim bowls, flagons, and mortaria. There is also some evidence for harder cream and grey fabrics (Plate 28).

Other industrial activity, such as textile and leather manufacture, was undoubtedly carried on in the *vicus* and perhaps at farms in the area, but no evidence for it has so far come to light. For most, the predominant occupation will have remained agricultural.

Rural settlement

The soldiers based in the fort at Lancaster and most of the occupants of the *vicus* were an anomaly in a population largely concerned with subsistence agriculture. Moreover they made the farmers' job harder as they represented an unproductive burden to be carried on the overall production of food. In particular the feeding of up to 500 cavalry horses and remounts, together with the transport animals required by the commissariat, must have aggravated the situation. The contents of the well on Castle Hill indicates the horses' diet (Jones and Shotter 1988,170–8; Plate 29).

The deposit in the well seemed to consist of a mixture of feed waste, both processed and unprocessed by horses, and stable litter. Analysis by Gay Wilson is most illuminating, as it demonstrates the wide variety of plant remains which had entered the horses' diet and bedding.

If it could be established that all these plants grew within the area of Lancaster they would have much to tell us about the landscape. However, there may well have been special-isation in sources of supply, and bulk supplies

Plate 29 The timber-lined well near the
east gate of the fort

may have been brought in from elsewhere (Manning 1975). We know all too little about the activities of the commissariat and most work has been angled at the diet of soldiers rather than their horses (Davies 1971).

Somewhat more reliable as an indication of local vegetation in Roman times is the analysis of pollen from north-western mosses (Oldfield and Statham 1964–5). This gives striking evidence for extensive pastoral activity with some arable in the fourth century AD, both in the southern Lake District and Cockerham Moss, which may be regarded as the extremes of Lancaster's *territorium*. At Foulshaw and Helsington Mosses, on the north side of Morecambe Bay, there is even a forest clearance phase during this same time, suggesting that there was considerable agricultural activity at the end of the Roman period.

It is likely that meat bones from both the *vicus* and the fort have much to tell us of local stock-rearing and butchering practices. The small samples so far available from stratified contexts limit the evidence, but published accounts (Jones and Shotter 1988, 167–9) are quite useful in showing the range. As would be expected ox, pig and sheep are well represented, but wild boar and deer almost certainly represent the results of hunting expeditions to the wild woods and moorlands. Surprisingly no study has been made to date of the fish and shellfish remains from Lancaster, which would almost certainly derive from the river Lune and Morecambe Bay. It is to be hoped that future work will amend this omission.

A number of specialised trades must have become centred on Lancaster, avoiding the need for every rural community to support every trade, again in agricultural terms largely unproductively.

It is plain that in many areas farmsteads must have approached very close to the forts, leading perhaps to a specialisation of output, rather like market-gardening around large cities. In Lancaster the evidence comes largely from isolated scatters of finds from within the present built-up area. Further out, comparatively little was known of rural settlement until the University of Lancaster's Lune Valley Survey and the programme of research for the production of a Lancashire Sites and Monuments Record radically altered the situation. Several sites of small farmsteads discovered in the nineteenth century and subsequently lost were rediscovered in the process, and many new sites were also located. Most of these survive as earthworks, never having been ploughed down. The pioneer work of Lowndes in the Lune Valley (Lowndes 1963, 77–95) indicated a fairly substantial survival of remains in that area, and this has been borne out by more recent work. Sites at Aughton, Leck, Claughton, and Tatham have been published recently (Howard-Davis 1983–4, 14–25). These appear to be small Romano-British farmsteads, but a site similarly categorised at Borwick proved upon excavation to be very much older (Olivier 1987b). Survey alone, therefore, needs to be used with caution, and only complete excavation can be considered reliable (Plates 30 and 31; Fig. 8)

In eastern Cumbria and in the area around Ingleton (Higham and Jones 1985, 68–98; King 1970, 53–80) a number of individual earthwork sites exist, and in some cases include subsidiary enclosures probably for sheep and cattle management. The Roman army, in particular, had heavy requirements for leather and skins as well as meat and grain.

The main problem is not just of locating rural settlement, but of dating it. It is virtually impossible to date farmsteads even within the Roman period, and in north Lancashire we are hampered by having no information at all on the Iron Age background. Thus, we cannot see what changes took place in the economy of the region as a result of the Roman conquest.

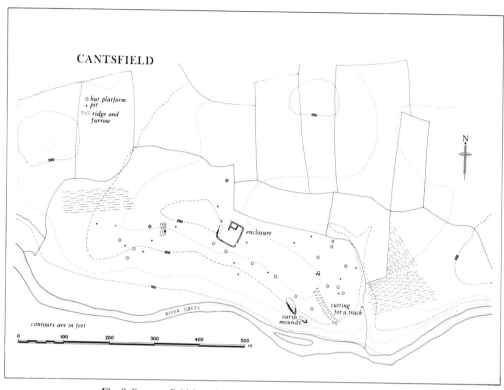

Fig. 8 Romano-British settlement at Cantsfield (Plan after R. C. Turner)

Plate 30 Romano-British settlement at Cantsfield

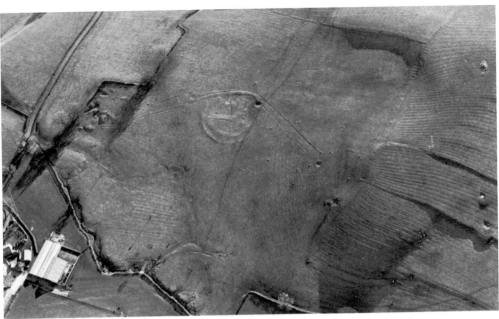

Plate 31 Probable Romano-British settlement at Sellet Hill (Photo: A. C. H. Olivier)

In these earthwork sites we are also seeing failed settlement – farmsteads on sites whose use did not continue. It is probable that many, even the majority of the ancient farmstead sites, with access to good pasture and water, are still occupied by modern farms.

One feature which the Lancaster area offered was a great variety of landscape – high fells to the east, and low wetlands to the west. The latter gave access no doubt to salt-making, wild-fowling and fishing, especially along the shores of Morecambe Bay.

There was also a considerable mineral wealth in the higher land, with coal, limestone, and iron ore, as well as stone for building and millstone grit for querns. The river Lune, navigable upstream at least as far as Lancaster, gave access to the produce of a wider world, and allowed the transport of goods not available locally.

8

CONCLUSION

Lancaster's Roman history has received much attention and has been well served by antiquarians, field-workers and excavators. Even so it has suffered from an approach that has been largely piecemeal, driven by the random availability of sites rather than by a programme designed to answer questions. At the time of writing, the city's largest excavation programme – in advance of redevelopment - is in train: it will undoubtedly provide evidence concerning the *vicus*, though still it is a response to a threat.

All the effort has elucidated a good deal concerning the nature of the Roman occupation: yet the foregoing pages will have served to emphasise the very significant gaps remaining in our knowledge. The nature and chronology of the military occupation are very imperfectly understood; even the location and extent of the forts are presumed from fragmentary evidence rather than from a reasonable amount of data.

The civilian settlement is known from stray finds and only a few, so far small, excavations – nothing that provides more than a slight clue to the sort of people who lived in the *vicus*, or the kinds of trades that they followed. Particularly, it is vital to discover how far their prosperity depended on their proximity to the river.

The surrounding countryside obviously responded to the new centre which the Roman site represented; the in-filling of the timber well excavated in 1973 provides some clues to an economic relationship, but they are clues which need to be put to the tests of fieldwork and excavation. Even the tileries and potteries of Quernmore,which have a good history of study, leave many unanswered questions about structure, extent and organization.

It is hoped that this book will have presented clearly the existing evidence and proposed some hypotheses which can be based on that evidence. In particular, it may have pointed towards the nature of some of the questions which need to be asked. It is, however, perhaps ironic that amongst such questions, we still have no answer to some very basic issues – when, why and how did the Romans first come to Lancaster, and how did their settlement fare in the increasing confusion that characterized the later years of the fourth century and the early years of the fifth?

Appendix 1

ROMAN INSCRIPTIONS FROM LANCASTER

The foregoing pages have made use of the evidence provided by the small body of epigraphic evidence from Lancaster; the purpose of the present section is to provide that evidence in full.

Most of the stone inscriptions are listed and discussed in *Roman Inscriptions of Britain* (*RIB*), although some more recent evidence is not included in that volume, nor is epigraphic material on tile or metal-work.

a) Inscriptions on Stone

i) *RIB* 600 (Plate 32). Found in 1802, beside the Lancaster–Kendal canal, south of Folly Farm (i.e. approximately one mile north of Lancaster). The altar is dedicated to the god, Jalonus Contrebis, presumably a meadow-land divinity associated with the river Lune. The element,

Plate 32 Inscription from Folly Farm (*RIB* 600; Lancaster Museum; Photo: Geoffrey Harris)

Contrebis, appears also on *RIB* 610 from Burrow-in-Lonsdale. The dedication is made by Julius Januarius, a retired decurion (i.e. a centurion in a cavalry unit), and, from the form in which the name is written, it is supposed to be not later than third century in date. The inscription's chief significance is the evidence which it may offer to the discussion of the Roman name for Lancaster (Chapter 4).

DEO | IALONO | CONTRE(bi) | SANCT[I]SS | MO IVLIV[S] | IANVARIVS | EM(eritus) EX DEC(urione) | V(otum) [S(olvit)]

To the most holy god, Jalonus Contrebis, Julius Januarius, retired former decurion, fulfilled his vow.

If the find-spot of the altar represents the location of the farm which Januarius was given after his discharge from service, it may be assumed that the vow is being fulfilled in return for a successful harvest. The altar is now in Lancaster City Museum.

ii) *RIB* 601 (Plate 33). Found in 1794 in the Churchyard at Halton-on-Lune. The altar is dedicated to the God, Mars, by Sabinus and his Irregular Unit of Bargemen; its chief significance lies in introducing into the Lancaster area a previously unknown unit of the Roman army. (For a discussion, see Shotter 1973, 206 and Chapter 5). The altar is broken down its right-hand side. It is possible that this altar is a 'carry' from Lancaster.

DEO | MART[I] | SABINV[S] | P(rae)P(ositus) ET MILIT[ES] | N(umeri) BARC(ariorum) S(ub) C(ura) | EIIVS PO[S](uerunt)

To the god, Mars, Sabinus, the commander, and the soldiers of the Unit of Bargemen under his command set this up.
The altar is in Lancaster City Museum.

iii) *RIB* 602 (Plate 34). Found in 1797 on the north side of the castle. The altar is dedicated to Mars Cocidius; the paralleling of a Celtic deity with his nearest equivalent in the Roman pantheon was common practice. In this case, Cocidius was presumably a war-god who has left evidence at a number of places in the north, though the chief centre of his cult appears to have been at Bewcastle (Fanum Cocidi). Lucius Vibenius, the dedicator, is described as *beneficiarius consularis*, which indicates a soldier seconded as an aide to the provincial governor's staff.

DEO | SANCTO MARTI | COCIDIO VIBENIVS | LVCIVS B(ene)F(iciarius) CO(n)S(ularis) | V(otum) S(olvit) L(ibens) M(erito)

Plate 33 Inscription from Halton (*RIB* 601; Lancaster Museum; Photo: Geoffrey Harris)

Plate 34 Inscription from Lancaster Castle (*RIB* 602; Lancaster Museum; Photo: Geoffrey Harris)

59

To the holy god Mars Cocidius, Lucius Vibenius, the governor's aide, willingly and deservedly fulfilled his vow. The altar is in Hadrian's Tower at Lancaster Castle.

iv) *RIB* 603. An altar stated to have been found around 1811 in a garden adjoining Vicarage Fields (Watkin 1883, 169f.). Its text is too weathered to permit reconstruction. The altar is now in Lancaster City Museum. It seems very likely that it is the same altar as that listed as *RIB* 607, which was found in Lancaster in 1753, reported by Stukeley, and subsequently lost.

Plate 35 Inscription from Lancaster Priory (*RIB* 604; Lancaster Museum; Photo: Geoffrey Harris)

v) *RIB* 604 (Plate 35). Top left-hand fragment of a dedication or building-stone found in the Priory Church in 1863. It is dedicated to the Emperor, Trajan, and presumably offers evidence that the fort (or part of it) was rebuilt in stone during that Emperor's reign (AD 98–117; cf. *RIB* 464 – Chester; *RIB* 665 – York).

IMP(eratori) NER(vae) | TRAIANO | AVG(usto) [GER(manico) DAC(ico)] | C [

To the Emperor, Nerva Trajan Augustus Germanicus Dacicus . . . Reconstruction is unsafe beyond this point. The stone is in Lancaster City Museum.

vi) *RIB* 605 (Plate 36). A dedication-stone, found in 1812 in a garden at the junction of Church Street and Bridge Lane, and fully discussed in Jones and Shotter 1988, 208 ff. It records the repair and rebuilding of a bath-house and basilica, which had collapsed through old age – often (though not necessarily) euphemistic language for the results of enemy action. A long-standing problem with this inscription – caused partly by the erasures (presumably) of an imperial name, and partly by the fact that the consuls, Censor and Lepidus, were unknown – was its date. Birley (1936, 5) has referred the period to that of the third century *Imperium Galliarum*, suggesting that the consuls fall into the period AD 262–266, vacant consular years in Postumus's reign. It is clearly a matter of some interest why such extensive repairs would be necessary at such a time; they could have resulted from a period of neglect, or from enemy action, or perhaps even civil strife. The bath-house to which the inscription refers has been located on the northern side of

Plate 36 The Bath-house inscription (*RIB* 605; Lancaster Museum; Photo: Geoffrey Harris)

Church Street, by its junction with Bridge Lane (Jones and Shotter 1988, 72 ff.). For its significance in the discussion of Lancaster's garrisons, see Chapter 5.

[/////////| OB] BALINEVM REFECT(um) | [ET] BASILICAM VETVSTATE CONLABSVM | A SOLO RESTITVTAM EQ(uitibus) ALAE SEBVSSIAN(ae) | //////// SVB OCTAVIO SABINO V(iro) C(larissimo) | PRAESIDE N(ostro) CVRANTE FLA(vio) AMMAV | SIO PRAEF(ecto) EQ(uitum) D(e)D(icata) XI KAL(endas) SEPTEM(bres) | CENSORE II ET LIPIDO II CO(n)S(ulibus)

The first erasure represents the Emperor's name and titles, the second an adjectival form of his name given honorifically to the *Ala Sebosiana*. (For the Emperor Postumus . . .) on account of the bath-house rebuilt and the basilica restored from ground-level, having collapsed through age, for the Cavalrymen of the *Ala Sebosiana* under the senator, Octavius Sabinus, our governor and Flavius Ammausius, the Prefect of Cavalry: dedicated on August 22nd in the year when Censor and Lepidus were consuls, each for the second time.

This stone came from a building recognised even before translation of the inscription as a bath-house. (*Lancaster Gazette* 7/3/1812). The basilica referred to is presumably a *Basilica Equestris Exercitatoria*, a drill-hall attached to the *Principia* of cavalry forts. This is presumably to be located beneath the Priory Church.

The stone is in Lancaster City Museum.

vii) *RIB* 606. A tombstone found in 1772 in Cheapside, and now lost. Its reading is based on contemporary drawings (Watkin 1883, 184; Edwards 1971, 23 ff.), and its date is likely to have been early in the second century. Apart from its find-spot, which possibly indicates a cemetery area, the stone's chief significance is in its reference to an *Ala Augusta*, which presumably (though not necessarily) had a period of garrison-duty at Lancaster. Like the *Ala Sebosiana* it was a Gallic unit, which 'justifies' the presence in it of Lucius Julius Apollinaris who came from Trier. For the *Ala Augusta*, see Chapter 5.

DIS MANI | BVS | L(ucius) IVL(ius) APOL | LINARIS | TREVER AN (norum) | XXX EQ(ues) AL | AE AV[G] | H(ic) [S(itus) E (st)]

Sacred to the Gods of the Underworld: Here lies Lucius Julius Apollinaris, from Trier, aged 30 years, a cavalryman in the *Ala Augusta*.

viii) *RIB* 607. (See above on *RIB* 603).

ix) *RIB* 608. Watkin (1883, 172) records this inscription as being on 'the base of a pillar', and as having been found at the junction of Church Street and Bridge Lane. Recently rediscovered drawings of the object show it to have been the base of a pipeclay statuette, and the inscription to have been a maker's mark – possibly that of Servandus of Cologne. It has been read as (Edwards 1971, 25 ff.):

SERVAN | DVS C(oloniae) C(laudiae) A(ugustae) A(grippinensium) | AD FORVM

Servandus, by the Forum at Cologne.
The actual findspot was Dr Wilson's house, 80 Church Street.

x) In March 1976, a fragment of an inscription was found in the disused rubbish tip at the western end of New Quay Road (Plate 37). The tip, which was closed towards the end of the nineteenth century, contained material which could be dated back to the middle of that century. We may assume, therefore, that the inscription came from one of the many mid-nineteenth-century redevelopment sites in Lancaster. The stone is in all probability a part of the right-hand side of a tombstone. It reads:

Plate 37 Fragment of an inscription from New Quay Road

[. . . . . .] I | [. . . . . ELICI | [. . . . . . OPATRI, and is perhaps a memorial to 'My Father, Felix'.

The stone remains in the finder's possesion (*Contrebis* IV (1976), 22 f.).

xi) *RIB* 616 and 617. These are inscriptions on the bases of two statuettes found on Cockersands Moss before 1718, and since lost. The Moss is a low-lying area of wetland lying 5 miles southwest of Lancaster.
Both are dedications to Mars Nodons (or Nodens). Nodons was a deity associated with the Irish Sea, who had a large temple at Lydney Park on the Severn estuary, which appears to have been built entirely in the second half of the fourth century (Lewis 1966, 139 ff.). The possible significance of the dedications for Lancaster is discussed in Jones and Shotter 1988, 217.

a)   DEO MARTI NODONTI AVR | ELIVS [. . . . .]CINVS SIG(illum) To the god, Mars Nodons, Aurelius . . . . . set up this statuette.
b)   D(eo) M(arti) N(odonti) | LVCIANVS | COLLEG(ae) APRILI VIATO | RIS V (otum) S(olvit)

To the god, Mars Nodons, Lucianus fulfilled the vow of his colleague, Aprilius Viator.
It is possible that all three men, Aurelius, Lucianus and Aprilius Viator were *milites* in the *Numerus Barcariorum*

b) Milestones

The Lancaster area has produced 3 milestones, all of which are in Lancaster City Museum.

i) *RIB* 2270. Found in 1811 at Burrow Heights, 3 miles south of Lancaster.

62

IMP(eratori) C(aesari) M(arco) IVLIO |
PHILIPPO | PIO FEL(ici) AVG(usto) |
N(ostro)

For the Emperor Caesar Marcus Julius
Philippus Pius Felix, our Augustus.
(AD 244–9).

ii) *RIB* 2271. Found in 1834, apparently close
to the find-spot of *RIB* 2270.

IMP(eratori) C(aesari) D(omino) N(ostro)
| GAIO MES [SIO] | QVINTO DECIO |
TRAIANO PIO FEL | ICI INVICTO AVG

For the Emperor Caesar, Our Lord, Gaius
Messius Quintus Decius Traianus Pius Felix
Invictus Augustus. (AD 249–251).

iii) *RIB* 2272 (Plate 38). Found in 1803 in the
Artle Beck, at Caton.

IMP(eratori) CAES(ari) | TR(aiano) HAD-
RIANO | AVG(usto) P(ontifici) M(aximo)
T(ribuniciae) P(otestatis) | CO(n)S(uli) III
P(atri) P(atriae) | L M(ilia) P(assuum) IIII

Plate 38 Milestone from the Artle Beck, Caton (*RIB*
2272; Lancaster Museum; Photo: Geoffrey Harris)

For the Emperor Caesar Traianus Hadrianus Augustus, Chief Priest, Holder of Tribunician
Power, Consul for the third time, Father of his Country (from . . .) four miles. AD 127–138).
For the significance of this stone in the discussion of Lancaster's Roman name, see Chapter 4.

c) Inscriptions and stamps on tiles and bricks (Figs. 9a and 9b)

The majority of known tile and brick stamps from Lancaster derived from the 1973 excavations
(Jones and Shotter 1988, 186 ff.). A group of five fragments contained portions of scored
inscriptions which appear to have read: ALSBVSA (for *Ala Sebosiana*). These are paralleled by
an unprovenanced fragment exhibited in 1752 to the Society of Antiquaries of London, and bearing
the inscription ALSB (*CIL* VII. 1240), which formed part of a tile tomb found 1752 and reported
to William Stukeley.

A fragment bearing the framed stamp,]BVSIA, was found in ditch-fill near the fort's east gate
in 1973, and appears to derive from the same die as the survivor (now in Lancaster Museum) of
those found in 1774 at Quernmore (*CIL* VII. 1233; Watkin 1883, 175–7. Watkin cites contemporary
evidence indicating a number of different stamps). The surviving specimen reads: ALE SEBVSIA
(for *Ala Sebosiana*).

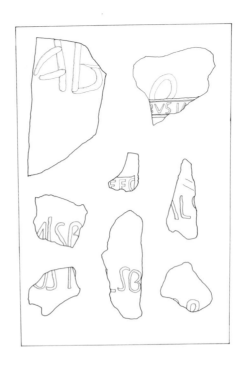

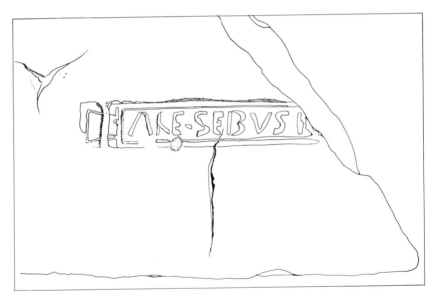

Figs. 9a and 9b Fragments of stamped, inscribed and impressed bricks and tiles (Lancaster Museum)

It is interesting that all the surviving evidence from Lancaster uses the form SEBVSIA(na) or SEBVSSIA(na), though the form SEBOSIANA appears on *CIL* XVI. 48 (Malpas Diploma), *ILS* 2533 (tombstone from Mainz) and *RIB* 1041 (from Bollihope Common, Co. Durham). The Malpas Diploma provides the full form, *Ala Gallorum Sebosiana*.

The 1973 excavations produced two further pieces from spots close to the fragment of the Wery Wall:

i)   a brick-stamp,] FEC(it), or '. . . made this'.

ii) a brick bearing an alphabetic graffito: AB[.

A further possible tile-stamp of the *Ala Sebosiana* was found on the Mitre Yard in 1974 (*Contrebis* III (1975), 53); it was very worn, but appeared to read]ESE[. .]S[, or ALESEBVSIA.

d) Lead Sealing (Fig. 10)

Found in 1973 on Western Vicarage Field (Jones and Shotter 1988, 152). The sealing carried in relief the letters ALS on the obverse face and IPD on the reverse. It seems likely the ALS stands for *Ala Sebosiana*, and IPD for a personal name (e.g. Iulius Primus) and the rank D(ecurio). One of the large group of sealings from Brough-under-Stainmore (Richmond 1936, 120) had ALASIIB on the obverse and VAL DEC on the reverse.

The sealing is in Lancaster City Museum.

Fig. 10 Lead Sealing of the *Ala Sebosiana* (Lancaster Museum)

Appendix 2

ROMAN COIN HOARDS FROM LANCASTER

Hoards of Roman coins are found all over Britain. Lancaster and its surrounding area have proved to be no exception to this, although it should be remembered that a distribution of find-spots is a reflection more of the modern activities that uncover them than it is of their concealment (Robertson 1974).

Although coins were deposited for different purposes, a true hoard represents usable savings and may consist of any number of coins from a single coin upwards – which have been deposited with the intention of recovery and use. In the absence of a banking-system, coins were stored securely to facilitate addition to and withdrawal from the deposit. It follows, therefore, that such a collection of money will not have been deposited far from the owner's centre of activity: under a floor, perhaps, or in a cist in the ground which could be easily recognized by the owner whilst remaining concealed from others. Within the hiding-place the coins might be stored in a variety of containers – pottery vessels, metal or wooden boxes, a 'purse' of leather or other material.

Coins were thus hoarded or 'banked' at all periods of the Roman occupation. But failure to remove them from their hiding-place (thus facilitating their discovery in modern times) might be due to individual circumstances, such as the sudden death or removal of the owner. This *might* in its turn be due to outside political or military events. Periods of economic uncertainty could induce people to attempt to retain 'good' money, or in times of economic change they could discard coins which reform had made useless. In Britain, although hoards terminating at all periods have been found, three 'peaks' occur: in the reign of Marcus Aurelius (*c.* AD 170), at the time of the *Imperium Galliarum* (*c.* AD 270), and again towards the close of the fourth century (Shotter 1978a).

The record of coin-hoards from Lancaster is, like that at most sites, very incomplete. In particular a few hoards have been found in the eighteenth and nineteenth centuries, when coins were rapidly dispersed, incompletely or inaccurately recorded, or perhaps selectively noticed by collectors. As a consequence, it is possible that hoard-coins have 'disappeared', only to re-emerge later robbed of their hoard-context (cf. Jones and Grealey 1974, 137 ff.). It is equally possible that separate accounts which appear to differ may in fact be describing the same hoard.

1   Watkin (1883, 188) records that in 1856 about 100 *Denarii* of the Early Empire were found during building work near the Wery Wall, 'at the bottom of Bridge Lane', which then followed a course from Covell Cross directly to St George's Quay, and was overlooked by the Wery Wall, as is shown on Mackreth's and Clark's maps of 1778 and 1807 respectively. The coins are said to have been rapidly dispersed although fourteen were subsequently acquired by Thomas Dalzell. In fact, the notebooks of Dalzell and another collector, Corbyn Barrow, which are lodged in Lancaster City Museum, show that the two men acquired nineteen of the

coins: Republican 5, Galba 1, Vespasian 8, Titus 3, Trajan 1, Hadrian 1 (fully listed in Jones and Shotter 1988, 202).

The date-range of the coins is 81BC–AD 118, and the presence of republican coins argues that the hoard will have contained few, if any, coins of later date (Reece 1974, 84). The hoard is of a group in Lancashire of which the latest coins are Trajanic or Hadrianic (Shotter 1978b). The two collectors differed as to whether the container was a pot or a box.

The discovery of the collectors' notebooks has allowed eleven of the coins to be relocated in the Lancaster City Museum's collection (*Contrebis* V (1977), 23–26).

2   Watkin (1883, 172) quotes from a letter from Fr Thomas West (dated February 1st, 1776) which gives details of a number of significant finds which appear to have been made at the western end of Church Street (near the present junctions with China Street and Bridge Lane: Lort 1779, 90 ff.; Penney 1981, 12). Amongst these was an apparent hoard, consisting of 'a great many Roman coins of Domitian, Vespasian etc', which was found beneath a stone during the digging of a cellar in a property on the south side of Church Street – perhaps near the present junction with Sun Street. If this was a hoard, it was most likely of a type which closed between AD 120 and 170.

3   Baines (1825, ii, 3) records the discovery during cellar-digging, evidently around the middle of the eighteenth century, of 'coins of Aelius, Hadrianus and Augustus Caesar'. The locality is not specified, nor is the status of the find clear.

4   The Alice Johnson Collection of papers (in Lancaster City Museum) contains two references to hoards. One is in the form of a letter (dated May 15th, 1908) to Alice Johnson from Reginald Smith (of the British Museum). In it Smith refers to a pot with coins, though no details are given, nor is it clear that it came from Lancaster. However, the find may be the same as that which features on a note in the papers referring to the acquisition by Mr Coupland of a perfect specimen of the Samian 'ink well' (Ritterling 13), which had been found 'full of early coins from near the Werry [sic] Wall'. This hoard could be the same as no. 1 above. 'Mr Coupland' may perhaps be Col Henry Coupland whose collection of prehistoric antiquities was given to the City Museum in 1938.

5   Thomas Cox (1720, 1295) refers to the discovery of imperial coins around 1700 'where the Friars had their cloister'. The Dominican Friary occupied an area astride the present Thurnham Street, to the east of Penny Street. No details of these coins exist elsewhere.

6   Watkin (1883, 188) records that in 1830 during the building of the Vicarage, a large number of coins was found, 'chiefly of Claudius, Vespasian, Domitian, Trajan, Hadrian, Antoninus Pius and Marcus Aurelius'. Many of the coins were acquired by Thomas Dalzell, and his notebooks show that many were *Aes* denominations. However, the find included four *Denarii* (one of Trajan and three of Antoninus). In the 1975 excavations on the same site four further *Denarii* were found (one each of Vespasian, Trajan, Hadrian and Marcus Aurelius as Caesar). Whilst there is no overt evidence that a hoard was involved, the presence of eight *Denarii* of

this date range at least prompts the suggestion that these coins may have represented part of a disturbed hoard (Jones and Shotter 1988, 203).

7 A hoard of fifteen radiates was found in North Vicarage Field in 1973 in the sub-floor debris of the *tepidarium* of the bath-house in the Courtyard Building.

There were nearby fragments of a black cooking-pot which may have been the container (Jones and Shotter 1988, 202). The hoard consisted of Gallienus 3, Postumus 1, Victorinus 5, Tetricus I 1, Claudius Tacitus 2, Carausius 1 (and two illegible coins).

8 A hoard (or part-hoard) of fifteen radiates was found in 1975 on the Mitre Yard (Jones and Shotter 1988, 202 f.), consisting of Gallienus 3, Claudius II 2, Postumus 1, Tetricus I 6, Tetricus II 1, Carausius 2.

9 Watkin (1883, 188) records the discovery in the churchyard earlier than 1836 of about 100 coins 'of Constantine and Probus', and specifies one issue of Constantius I as Caesar (Jones and Shotter 1988, 203). If this was a hoard, it was presumably of the type containing 'reformed' radiates and tetrarchic 'reformed' issues (*c.* AD 275–300). The decline in the coinage after AD 300 prompted such hoarding of better quality earlier coins (Reece 1974, 93), and the present collection is in the north-west paralleled at Kirksteads (Casey 1978, 50–55; Shotter and James 1984, 260–62) and at Cliburn (Shotter 1986, 250–5).

10 Lancaster City Museum has a record of about thirty coins which were recovered from Albert Square (now covered by the Mitre House complex) prior to 1931. No details were recorded. It is quite possible that this information is a separate record of hoard 1.

The area around Lancaster has produced only one certain hoard, together with two finds which *may* be hoards:

(a) Between 1975 and 1980, 123 debased radiates were found in the bank of the river Keer on Docker Moor (Shotter 1982, 198 f.). These consisted of Gallienus 9, Claudius II 12, Postumus 1, Victorinus 17, Tetricus I 53, Tetricus II 15, together with 16 illegible coins. Although there was no sign of a container, a dark deposit on some of the coins may represent the perished remains of a leather purse.

(b) Two *Denarii* of the reign of Alexander Severus, found at Silverdale in 1970, may represent a hoard or a votive deposit (Shotter 1972, 333 f.).

(c) Reference should be made to a group of 77 coins presented for examination in 1977, which *may* have come from the Lancaster area. It has to be said, however, that neither the provenance nor the status of the coins can be regarded as reliable. The coins range from Alexander Severus to Gratian, and consist of Alexander Severus 1, Gallienus 2, Claudius II 2, Victorinus 1, Tetricus I 9, Tetricus II 6, Radiates 3, Allectus 1, Constantine I 39, Constans 2, Constantius II 4, Valens 1, Valentinian 2, Gratian 2 (and 2 illegible coins). Details and discussion are to be found in *Contrebis* VII (1979–80), 34–37.

Appendix 3

ROMAN COINS FROM LANCASTER

As with most Roman sites, the quality of information on Roman coins is very variable. It is clear that over the years hoards and other substantial collections of coins have been found, as well as more isolated coins. Much of this discovery occurred during building work in the eighteenth and nineteenth centuries before the existence of the great Roman coin Concordances made identification generally so much easier. Further, much of the material was rapidly dispersed into collections which have either now totally disappeared or at least obscured the original circumstances of discovery. It is likely also that the part played by coin *collectors* has meant that a greater emphasis was placed upon the better preserved and more pleasing specimens to the detriment of the often unimpressive, but no less significant, material of third- and fourth-century date.

Despite such problems, however, Lancaster has proved more fortunate than some sites. Two of the chief nineteenth-century collectors, Thomas Dalzell and Corbyn Barrow, were meticulous over their recording of specimens which came into their possession. Further, the discovery of their notebooks in Lancaster City Museum has allowed many items of their collections to be re-identified amongst the Museum's coins. Also Watkin (1883, 189–192) attempted to compile a record of known coins from Lancaster at a time when their locations were still open to discovery. His coin list continues to provide the foundation for any review of the coin evidence, particularly since he had access to the material belonging to local collectors other than Dalzell and Barrow.

In more recent years, recording has been sounder; casual finds from around the city have been recorded by the City Museum, and major excavations have yielded a considerable number of coins whose contexts are obviously beyond dispute and uncertainty (Jones and Shotter, 1988, 189 ff.). As a result the Roman coin sample for Lancaster reaches approximately 300, providing a good basis for a discussion of the implications of coin loss evidence.

Although coins have been reported from many areas of the city, Watkin's account (1883, 188) makes it clear that certain areas have yielded large numbers:

1. Church Street (leading from the East gate through an area of known *vicus* occupation)
2. The Old Vicarage
3. The Churchyard
4. The Station

(both of these represent locations from the interior of the fort)

In short, the general distribution of coin finds, with a comparatively small number coming from the southern and western sides of the fort, would suggest that the principal areas of activity were Castle Hill itself, and an area to the north and east, perhaps contained between a road out of the north gate of the fort, the river and Church Street.

69

The following table attempts to provide fort and *vicus* locations for the known coins

Table I: Distribution of Lancaster's Roman Coins into Issue-Periods.

	Fort	N/E *Vicus*	Other *Vicus* Locations	?	Total	%
I (–AD 41)	2		1	2	5	1.59
II (41–54)	1	2		1	4	1.27
III (54–69)	4			1	5	1.59
IV (69–96)	12	9	1	3	25	7.96
V (96–117)	15	6	1	3	25	7.96
VI (117–138)	5	2	1	4	12	3.82
VII (138–161)	12	6	4	3	25	7.96
VIII (161–180)	6	5		6	17	5.41
IX (180–192)	1	1	2	1	5	1.59
X (192–222)	3	1		3	7	2.23
XI (222–235)				1	1	0.32
XII (235–259)	5		1	1	7	2.23
XIII (259–275)	35		3	15	53	16.88
XIV (275–294)	4			13	17	5.41
XV (294–324)	18	3		14	35	11.16
XVI (324–330)	1				1	0.32
XVII (330–346)	25	2		8	35	11.16
XVIII (346–364)	10	1		3	14	4.46
XIX (364–378)	7		2	4	13	4.14
XX (378–388)	1		1	2	4	1.27
XXI (388–)				4	4	1.27
	167	38	17	92	314	

Table II: Denominations (Periods I–XII)

	AV	AR Ant	Den	AE Sest	Dup	As	?	Total
I			3	1	1			5
II			2				2	4
III			2		1	2		5
IV			6	3	2	4	10	25
V			3	7		6	9	25
VI			3	1	1	2	5	12
VII			6	2	3	3	11	25
VIII			3	4	3	4	3	17
IX			1		1	1	2	5
X			4	1		1	1	7
XI				1	1			1
XII		3		3	1			7
		3	31	24	14	23	43	138

Table III: As-equivalent value (Periods I–XII)

I	54
II	8
III	36
IV	116
V	82
VI	56
VII	113
VIII	74
IX	19
X	69
XI	2
XII	110

Table IV: Mints of origin of the Fourth-Century Coins

	XV	XVI	XVII	XVIII	XIX	XX	XXI
LONDON	4						
TRIER	9	1	13	6	4	1	1
ARLES	1		3	1	2	1	1
LYONS	2		7				1
AQUILEIA					1		
SISCIA						1	
CARTHAGE	1						
CYZICUS				1			
?	15		11	6	6	1	1

It should be noted that the Mitchells Brewery Site Excavations of 1988 yielded 34 coins (that is, from a north-east *vicus* area); preliminary study suggests that of these 24 derive from XIII or later. This would suggest that with regard to the north-east *vicus* area the figures in Table I are misleading. The majority of coins from the fort from Periods XIII and later come from recent excavations, whilst prior to 1988 few excavations had taken place on north-east *vicus* sites: indeed, those that had were mainly on small sites fronting Church Street, where later Roman deposits have probably been destroyed by cellar construction. It would appear that away from street frontages a much longer Roman sequence of occupation survives. It is probably also the case that the scarcity of later coins from north-east *vicus* sites reflects the interests of collectors – alluded to above. It is therefore more appropriate to reserve judgement on occupation in various parts of the city rather than, as has been the case in studies of Lancaster and elsewhere, to construct hypotheses concerning apparently short-lived *vicus* occupation (Shotter 1985, 91 ff.).

Discussion (Fig. 11)

Of the total coin sample from Lancaster, approximately 30% cannot be assigned a certain provenance within the city: of the remainder some 75% derive from fort locations, and 25% from extramural areas.

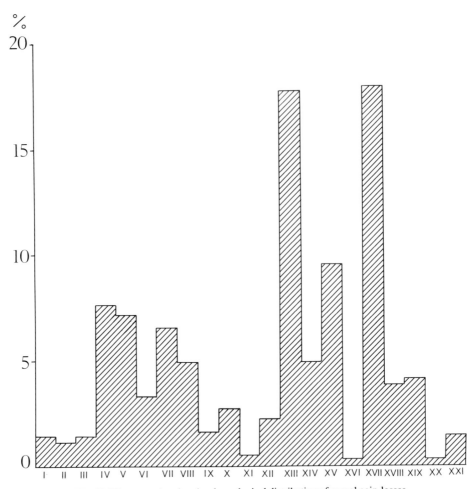

Fig. 11 Histogram showing the chronological distribution of casual coin-losses

The Chronology of Occupation

The distribution of Lancaster's Roman coins into issue-periods is shown on Table I. It should be noted that the coins have displayed varying degrees of wear, and since it is known that Roman coins often enjoyed long periods of circulation, the *issue-dates* may not always provide a reliable indication of the dates of loss.

The first substantial group of coins from both fort and *vicus* locations comes from the Flavian period (IV), although a not inconsiderable number of pre-Flavian coins is represented in the sample. The significance of such pre-Flavian issues is hard to assess: silver coins might well persist in circulation into the late first century, whilst bronze/copper issues were less long-lived: due to the successful reorganisation of minting activities by Vespasian, the later first century was much better supplied with current coinage. However, even if some early coins – for example, *denarii* of M. Antonius – persist in circulation for very long periods, it is likely that some at least of Lancaster's pre-Flavian issues represent some pre-Agricolan activity. As suggested above (on p. 17), a context for some kind of military intervention in Neronian or early Flavian times might be provided by the disturbed state of Brigantian politics in the 60s. There is of course no indication of the location of any site in the Lancaster area which might be associated with such activity.

The samples of Flavian and Trajanic coins (IV and V) are numerically closely similar. It is normal for Agricolan sites (for example, Ribchester (Shotter 1985)) to display a marked preponderance of Flavian over Trajanic issues. The relationship between IV and V at Lancaster should be explained by a factor affecting Flavian coin loss - perhaps a short break in occupation in the AD 90s. A context for this might be found in the frontier arrangements on the Stanegate which required attention at that time (Jones 1982). Considerable coin loss in the Flavian and Trajanic periods is also evidenced in *vicus* areas, suggesting that an extra-mural settlement was established rapidly in the wake of the military site.

Occupation was clearly maintained through the Trajanic and Hadrianic periods. However, the sample shows a sharp drop in the loss of Hadrianic coins (VI). These issues would bulk largest in circulation in the early Antonine period, and the low showing of such coins would point to an interruption in occupation at that time. A context is readily found in the reoccupation of southern Scotland in the early 140s.

From the Antonine period (VII) onwards, coin loss was progressively affected by economic and monetary factors: rising inflation rendered the 'small change' increasingly redundant, and circulating money was dominated by *denarii* and *sestertii*, supplemented under Caracalla by the inflationary *antoninianus* or double-*denarius*. Normally, therefore, those who lost these higher value coins will have searched more carefully for them. Thus coin loss generally tends to decrease through VII, VIII and IX. Whilst this is the case at Lancaster, it is worth noting that a considerable number of coins is involved. We may, therefore, assume that, following a break in occupation in the early Antonine period, Lancaster was reoccupied after the final withdrawal from Scotland *c.* AD 165, and shared with other sites in the north-west a period of reconstruction (Potter 1979) in both fort and *vicus*.

Severan coins (X) are poorly represented in the Lancaster sample, with only one certainly provenanced from the *vicus*. Indeed, it was thought at one time that the *vicus* had undergone major changes, with perhaps abandonment in the later second century. Recent excavations, however, have shown that this was a misleading impression, and that most sampling had been restricted to places where significant post-Roman disturbance had occurred. The poor showing of Severan coins is followed by an equally small number from Period XI. This might indicate a further break in occupation in the early third century, particularly since the sample recovers in XII, and the middle of the century is marked by evidence of reconstruction – two milestones of the 240s and the rebuilding of the basilica and bath-house in the 260s (*RIB* 605).

As is usual on Roman sites in north-west England, the middle of the century (XIII) shows large scale coin loss at Lancaster in both fort and *vicus*. These coins consist of regular issues and local ('barbarous') copies, though Lancaster had yielded fewer copies of very poor quality than have some other sites. It is not clear how long such coins remained in circulation, though they clearly dominated regular issues of the later 270s and 280s – until supplemented by issues of Carausius and Allectus (AD 287–296). There is in fact evidence from some sites that radiates and copies continued to circulate alongside current issues well into the fourth century. The mid-third century was a period of anarchy in the Empire, with the west split between the legitimate emperors

(Gallienus and Claudius II) and the usurpers of the 'Empire of the Gauls' (Postumus, Victorinus and the Tetrici). The Lancaster sample shows a reasonably even division between legitimate rulers and usurpers.

Occupation evidently continued uninterrupted into the fourth century with all periods (XV–XIX) well represented. This serves to indicate the new importance of Lancaster as a fort for coastal defence. Coins of the House of Valentinian constituted the last large-scale element in the money supply in northern Britain, with new issues beyond AD 378 (XX and XXI) generally sparsely supplementing worn issues of earlier parts of the century. Even so, it is worth noting that the number of coins from XX and XXI is relatively large, and (unusually) XXI is as well represented as XX. Throughout the fourth century, the coins from Lancaster are predominantly regular issues (rather than local copies); further, in those cases where the mint mark can be read (Table IV), this is seen to show that the coins originated from the western mints, suggesting that their origin was military pay.

The coin evidence therefore suggests that military activity at Lancaster was sustained throughout the fourth century, and probably into the early years of the fifth, emphasising the continued importance of west-coast naval defence (Potter 1979, 364 ff.). Further, in the light of the most recent (1988) excavations, it is now possible to say that the *vicus* too survived well into the fourth century.

The Nature of the Occupation

Inscriptions demonstrate that Lancaster's garrison was for considerable periods at least made up of cavalry units. Different units were paid at different rates, and their pay will therefore have been made up by different denominations. The relatively highly paid cavalry units might therefore be expected to betray their presence through a preponderance of higher value coins over lower.

Although in many cases the Roman coins from Lancaster have not been sufficiently completely recorded to allow determination of the denomination, the sample for Periods I–XII (the 'period of the *denarius*') shows a marked preponderance of *denarii* and *sestertii* over the smaller denominations. Whilst by the middle of the second century AD, monetary factors tended to produce this phenomenon, it is also clear for earlier periods too. Although the sample of fully recorded coins is too low for certainty, it can be said that the denominational distribution (Table II) would support the presence in Lancaster of a higher paid (that is, cavalry) unit.

Vicus Coins

We have, of course, an incomplete picture. However, the distribution of coin finds emphasises the significance of the line of Church Street and the area between it and the river. Thus the area around the fort's north-east quarter would, on present evidence, appear to be the focus of *vicus* activity. Further, as we have seen, despite earlier impressions that *vicus* occupation might have been shortlived, it is now clear that the overall period of occupation in this area closely matches that of the fort. Indeed, it is likely that in the fourth century, with the building of the new fort on the north and east slopes of Castle Hill, the importance of this area may have received new emphasis.

Several coins (Table I) have been found on the south and west sides of the fort, and at distances of up to a mile from Castle Hill. This indicates the likelihood of a certain amount of dispersed settlement perhaps merging into a landscape of small farms in the hinterland of the fort.

COIN LIST

(*denotes that a coin derives from an excavation)

i)	*Republican* (–31 BC)						
	Denarius *Crawford*		372.1	81 BC			
	Denarius		544	32–1 BC	Cannon Hill	1873	
	Denarius		544	32–1 BC	Old Vicarage	1975 *	
ii)	*Augustus* (31 BC–AD 14)						
	Sestertius						
	Dupondius	*RIC*	68 etc.	23 BC	Old Vicarage	1830	
iii)	*Claudius* (AD 41–54)						
	Sestertius	*RIC*	65	41–54			
	Sestertius		62	41–54	Old Vicarage	1830	
	?			41–54	Fleet Square	1853	
	?			41–54	Church Street	1853	
iv)	*Nero* (AD 54–68)						
	Denarius	*RIC*	56	64–68	Wery Wall	1928 *	
	As		329	54–68	Old Vicarage	1830	
	As		329	54–68			
v)	*Galba* (AD 68–69)						
	Dupondius	*RIC*	64	68–69	Old Vicarage	1830	
vi)	*Otho* (AD 69)						
	Denarius	*RIC*	12	69	St Mary Gate	1834	
vii)	*Vespasian* (AD 69–79)						
	Denarius	*RIC*	287	70–71	Old Vicarage	1975 *	
	Denarius		10	69–71	N. Vicarage Field	1974 *	
	Denarius		30	70–72	N. Vicarage Field	1973 *	
	Denarius		67	73			
	Sestertius		42	71	Old Vicarage	1830	
	Sestertius		516	72–73	Old Vicarage	1830	
	?			69–79	Churchyard	1836	
	?			69–79	Station	1849	
	?			69–79	Church Street	1854	

75

viii) *Domitian* (AD 81–96)

Denarius	*RIC*	147	90		
Denarius			81–96	New Quay Road	1981
Sestertius		318	86	Churchyard	
Dupondius		327	86	Churchyard	1830
Dupondius		381	88	Old Vicarage	1830
As			84–96	Mitre Yard	1973
As			84–96	78 Church Street	1978 *
As			86–96	Cheapside	1984 *
As			81–96	Quernmore Road	1981 *
(AE)			81–96		*c.* 1862
?			81–96	Churchyard	1853
?			81–96	Church Street	1853
?			81–96	Church Street	1853
?			81–96	Fleet Square	1853
?			81–96	Churchyard	1836
?			81–96	Churchyard	1837–8

ix) *Nerva* (AD 96–98)

Sestertius			96–98	Castle Hill	1975
As	*RIC*	84	97	Mitre Yard	1974
?			96–98	Long Marsh Lane	1965
(AE)			96–98	Castle	*c.* 1800

x) *Trajan* (AD 98–117)

Denarius	*RIC*	165	103–111	Old Vicarage	1830
Denarius			98–117		1752
Denarius			98–117	Old Vicarage	1975 *
Sestertius			103–117	Castle Hill (?)	1975
Sestertius			103–117	Castle Hill (?)	1975
Sestertius		560	103–111	Old Vicarage	1830
Sestertius		475	103–111	Old Vicarage	1830
Sestertius		476	103–111		
Sestertius		675	114–117	Old Vicarage	1830
As		392	98–99	Old Vicarage	1830
As			98–102	78 Church Street	1975 *
As		549	103–111	Mitre Yard	1974
As			98–117		1973 *
?			98–117	Churchyard	1853
?			98–117	Church Street	1854
?			98–117	China Street	1906
?			98–117	Church Street	1854
?			98–117	Church Street	1854
?			98–117		
?			98–117	Church St/New St	

xii)	*Hadrian* (AD 117–138)					
	Denarius			134–138	Old Vicarage	1975 *
	Denarius			117–138		1985
	Denarius	*RIC*	80 ff.	119–122	Aldcliffe	1988
	Sestertius			117–138	Old Vicarage	1830
	As		667	125–128	Churchyard	1869
	As		668	125–128	Mitre Yard	1973*
	?			117–138	Churchyard	1836
	?			117–138		
	? (L. Aelius)			134–137		
	?			117–138	Church St/New St	
	Dupondius			117–138		
	?			117–138	Church St/New St	1868
xii)	*Antoninus Pius* (AD 133–161)					
	Denarius			138–161	Church Street	1809
	Denarius			138–161	Old Vicarage	1830
	Denarius			138–161	Old Vicarage	1830
	Denarius			138–161	Old Vicarage	1830
	Denarius			138–161		1984
	Denarius (Marcus Caesar)	*RIC*	422	140–144	Old Vicarage	1975 *
	Sestertius		605	140–144		
	Sestertius			138–161	North Vicarage Field	1974 *
	Dupondius			138–161	Castle Hill (?)	*c.* 1965
	As		685	140–144	Priory Church	1929
	As		819	145–161	Old Vicarage	1830
	As		934	154–155	Churchyard	pre-1850
	(AE)			139	Church Street	1854
	?			138–161	Churchyard	1837–8
	?			138–161	Union Square	1854
	?			138–161	Churchyard	*c.* 1836
	?			138–161	Church Street	1906
	?			138–161	King Street	1854
	(Faustina I)					
	Dupondius	*RIC*	1090	138–141		
	Dupondius			141+	North Vicarage Field	1974
	(AE)			138+	Church Street	1809
	?			138+	Fleet Square	1853
	?			138+	Edward Street	1854
	?			138+	West Road	*c.* 1908
	?			138+	West Road	*c.* 1908
xiii)	*Marcus Aurelius* (AD 161–180)					
	Denarius (Lucilla)					*c.* 1876

	Sestertius			161–180	Church Street	1776
	Sestertius			151–180		
	Sestertius			161–180		
	Dupondius	*RIC*	1040	171–172	Castle Hill (?)	*c.* 1965
	Dupondius (Verus)			161–169		
	As		1089	172–173	Old Vicarage	1830
	As		1089	172–173	Old Vicarage	1830
	?			161–180	Churchyard	*c.* 1836
	?			161–180	Union Square	1854
	(Faustina II*)*					
	Denarius	*RIC*	705	161–176		
	Denarius		746	176–180	Church Street	1776
	Sestertius		1651	161–176	Church Street	1983
	Dupondius			161–176	North Vicarage Field	1974
	As		1647	161–176	Mitre Yard	1973 *
	?			161–176	Church Street	1972
xiv)	*Commodus* (AD 180–192)					
	Dupondius			180–192	Cannon Hill	1985
	As	*RIC*	293	179–180		
	?			180–192	Churchyard	*c.* 1836
	As			180–192	41 Church Street	1975
	(Crispina)					
	Denarius	*RIC*	283	180		*c.* 1850
	?			180	Springfield Street	1950
xv)	*Septimius Severus* (AD 193–211)					
	Denarius	Hill	560	202	Castle Hill (?)	*c.* 1965
	Denarius	Hill	306	198		1752
	Sestertius			193–198	Castle Hill (?)	*c.* 1965
	As	*RIC*	791	209	Old Vicarage	1830
	?			193–211		
	(Julia Domna)					
	Denarius			193–211	Church St/New Rd	1868
xvi)	*Caracalla* (AD 198–217)					
	Denarius			198–217		
xvii)	*Alexander Severus* (AD 222–235)					
	Dupondius/As	*RIC*	643/4	231–235		

xviii)	*Maximinus* (AD 235–238)				
	Sestertius	*RIC*	49	235–238	Castle Railway Station	1982
	Sestertius		90	236–238	Churchyard	1830
	Dupondius/As (Maximinus Caesar)			235–238	Churchyard	1836
xix)	*Gordian III* (AD 238–244)				
	Antoninianus	*RIC*	156	243–244	Vicarage Field	1978
	Sestertius		258a or 262a	238–239		
xx)	*Volusian* (AD 251–253)				
	Antoninianus	*RIC*	140	253	W. Vicarage Field	1972 *
xxi)	*Valerian* (AD 253–259)				
	Antoninianus			253–259	W. Vicarage Field	1972 *
xii)	*Gallienus* (AD 253–268)				
		RIC	157	259–269		
			157	259–268		
			179	259–268	N.Vicarage Field	1973 *
			317	259–268	N. Vicarage Field	1973 *
			249	259–268	Mitre Yard	1974
			226	259–268	N. Vicarage Field	1974
			465a	259–268	N. Vicarage Field	1974
			157	259–268	N. Vicarage Field	1974
			216	259–268	N. Vicarage Field	1974
			326	259–268	N. Vicarage Field	1974
			320	259–268	N. Vicarage Field	1976
	(*Salonina*)			253–268	N. Vicarage Field	1958 *
xxiii)	*Claudius II* (AD 268–270)				
		RIC	35	268–270	N. Vicarage Field	1974
			43	268–270	N. Vicarage Field	1974
			49	268–270	W. Vicarage Field	1929 *
			265	270		
				268–270	Castle Hill (?)	*c.* 1965
				268–270	Mitre Yard	1973 *
xxiv)	*Postumus* (AD 260–268)				
		RIC	59	260–268		
			59	260–268		
			59	260–268		
			80	260–268		
			80	260–268		

			89	260–268	W. Vicarage Field	1972 *
			93	260–268	N. Vicarage Field	1974
			66	260–268		1755
			260	268		1985
			260	268		
			260	268	Quernmore Road	1979
xxv)	*Victorinus* (AD 269–271)					
		RIC	118	269–271		
			53	269–271	N. Vicarage Field	1973
			114	269–271	W. Vicarage Field	1929 *
			122	269–271	Ashton Road	1976
			114	269–271	N. Vicarage Field	1977 *
				269–271	Nelson Sreet	1966
				269–271	N. Vicarage Field	1974 *
xxvi)	*Tetricus* 1 (AD 271–273)					
		RIC	76/7	271–273		
			76/7	271–273		
				271–273		1985
				271–273	N. Vicarage Field	1975 *
			76/7	271–273	W. Vicarage Field	1929 *
				271–273	Churchyard	1853
				271–273	Castle Hill	1956
			76	271–273	N. Vicarage Field	1974
				271–273	W. Vicarage Field	1971 *
			87	271–273	Mitre Yard	1974
				271–273	Castle Hill (?)	*c.* 1965
xxvi)	*Tetricus II* (AD 271–273)					
				271–273	N. Vicarage Field	1974 *
xxvii)	*Illegible Radiates and Copies*					
				c. 270	N. Vicarage Field	1973 *
				c. 270	W. Vicarage Field	1971 *
				c. 270	Mitre Yard	1973
				c. 270	Mitre Yard	1973
				c. 270	Old Vicarage	1975 *
xxviii)	*Probus* (AD 276–282)					
		RIC	118/9	276–282		
			343	276–282	N. Vicarage Field	1974
xxix)	*Carausius* (AD 287–293)					
		RIC	33 (?)	287–293		
			33 (?)	287–293		
			34/35	287–293		

			101	288–289	N. Vicarage Field	1973
			101	288–289	Castle Parade	1860
			284 ff	287–293		1985
			300	287–293		
			300	287–293		
			300	287–293		
			696	287–293	N. Vicarage Field	1973

xxx)   *Allectus* (AD 293–296)

		RIC	28	293–296		
			28	293–296		
			128–130	293–296		

xxxi)   *Diocletian* (AD 283–306)
RIC

| | | (Tripolis) | 327 | 285 | | 1975 |
| | | (Trier) | 511 | 294–306 | N. Vicarage Field | 1973 * |

GENIO POPVLI ROMANI   294–306

| | | | | 284–306 | Churchyard | *c.* 1836 |
| | | | | 284–306 | Priory Church | 1914 |

xxxii)   *Maximian* (AD 286–308)
GENIO POPVLI ROMANI   294–306   N. Vicarage Field   1974
GENIO POPVLI ROMANI   294–306

xxxiii)   *Constantius I* (AD 293–306)
GENIO POPVLI ROMANI   294–306
GENIO POPVLI ROMANI   294–306

xxxiv)   *Maxentius* (AD 306–312)

| | | *RIC* (Carthage) | 60 | 307 | Old Vicarage | 1830 |

xxxv)   *Licinius* (AD 308–324)

| | | *RIC* (Trier) | 845b | 310–313 | | |
| | | | | 310–313 | | |

xxxvi)   *Constantine I and family* (AD 307–346)

		RIC (Trier)	725	307	N. Vicarage Field	1973 *
				313+	N. Vicarage Field	1974
				313+	Church Street	1854
				313+	W. Vicarage Field	1971 *
				313+	Mitre Yard	1974
				313+	St George's Quay	1973
				313+	China Street	1906

SOLI INVICTO COMITI		313–317		
(London)	154	319	W. Vicarage Field	1971 *
(Trier)	208A	318–319	N. Vicarage Field	1974
as (Trier)	208A	318–319	Castle Hill (?)	c. 1965
(Trier)	253	320	N. Vicarage Fieid	1974
(Arles)	208	320–321	N. Vicarage Field	1974
(London)	pp 110–5	321–324		
(London)	pp 110–5	321–324		
(London)	pp 110–5	321–324		
(Trier)	pp 190–201	321–324		
(Trier)	pp 190–201	321–324		
as (Trier)	303	321	W. Vicarage Field	1971 *
(Lyons)	132	321	N. Vicarage Field	1977
(Lyons)	pp 131–4	321–323		
(Trier)	441	323–324	N. Vicarage Field	1975
as (London)	291	323–324	Castle Hill (?)	c. 1965
(Trier)	431			
as (*LRBC* I.26)	324–330		Churchyard	

GLORIA EXERCITVS (– 2 std)				
LRBC	1.48	330–335	Castle Hill (?)	c. 1965
	56	330–335	Old Vicarage	1975 *
	49	330–335	N. Vicarage Field	1973 *
	48	330–335	N. Vicarage Field	1973 *
	49	330–335	St George's Quay	1979
		330–335	N. Vicarage Field	1970 *
		330–335	N. Vicarage Field	1970 *
		330–335	Castle	1980
		330–335	N. Vicarage Field	1970 *
		330–335	N. Vicarage Field	1972 *
		330–335	Mitre Yard	1974

GLORIA EXERCITVS (– 1 std)				
	102/3	337–341		
	252	337–341	Mitre Yard	1973 *
		335–341	N. Vicarage Field	

(Victory on prow)				
	185	330–335		
	185	330–335		
	185	330–335		
	185	330–335		
	191	330–335	Mitre Yard	1973 *
	71	330–335	St George's Quay	1979

(She–wolf and twins)				
	355	330–335		
	355	330–335		
	355	330–335		
	51	330–335	N. Vicarage Field	1974
	51	330–335	N. Vicarage Field	1974 *
	190	330–335	N. Vicarage Field	1973 *
		330–335	W. Vicarage Field	1972 *
		330–335	N. Vicarage Field	1974
		330–335	W. Vicarage Field	1929 *
(Quadriga)				
	114	337–341	N. Vicarage Field	1977 *
VICTORIAE D D AVGG Q N N				
	148	341–346	N. Vicarage Field	1973 *
	148	341–346	N. Vicarage Field	1973 *
	148	341–346	N. Vicarage Field	1974 *
	257	341–346	Old Vicarage	1975 *

xxxvii) *Constans/Constantius II* (AD 346–364)

LRBC II.29 (Hut)	346–350	N. Vicarage Field	1974
29 (Hut)	346–350	N. Vicarage Field	1974
29 (Hut)	346–350	N. Vicarage Field	1974
(Hut)	346–350	W. Vicarage Field	1929 *
33 (Phoenix)	346–350		
(Phoenix)	346–350	Old Vicarage	1975 *
2496 (Horseman)	351–354		1978
460	355–360	N. Vicarage Field	1974
	346–364	Vicarage Field	1853
	346–364	Priory Church	1912
	346–364	St George's Quay	1956
	346–364	Mitre Yard	1974

xxxviii) *Magnentius* (AD 351–353)

62	351–353	Castle	*c.* 1908
62	351–353		

xxxix) *Valentinianic* (AD 364–388)

Siliqua VRBS ROMA	364–375		1752
LRBC II. 97	367–375	Mitre Yard	1974
96	367–375	W. Vicarage Field	1971 *
96	367–375	Mitre Yard	1973 *
97	367–375	W. Vicarage Field	1971 *
521	367–375		

		528	367–375	Hillside	
SECVRITAS			367–375	Meeting House Lane	1861
REIPVBLICAE		965	364–375		1978
			364–375		
			364–375	Castle	1944
			364–375	W. Vicarage Field	1973
			367–375	Mitre Yard	1974
Siliqua *RIC* (Trier)		61	378–383	Old Vicarage	1975 *

xl) *Valentinian II* (AD 378–392)

| *LRBC* | II.1541 | 378–383 | Cleveleys Avenue | 1984 |

xli) *Theodosius* (AD 379– 395)

| *LRBC* | II.565 | 388–392 |
| VIRTVS ROMANORVM (?) | | 378–383 |

xlii) *Arcadius* (AD 383–408)

| *LRBC* | II.167 | 388–392 |

xliii) *Honorius* (AD 393–423)

| *LRBC* | II.396 | 394–395 |
| | | 393–402 |

Coins from Lancaster's Hinterland

A. A number of coins have been recorded from areas which are within the present city, though outside the presumed fort and *vicus* areas of the Roman site. Such finds may well be indicative of farm–sites close to the Roman site itself.

Aldcliffe	1988	Denarius of Hadrian (*RIC* 80 ff.)	119–122
Ashton Road	1976	Radiate copy of Victorinus (*RIC* 122)	269–271
Cannon Hill	1873	Denarius of M. Antonius	32–1 BC
	1985	Dupondius of Commodus	180–192
Cleveleys Avenue	1984	AE of Valentinian II (*LRBC* II.1541)	378–383
Edward Street	1854	Faustina I	138+
Marsh Lane	1849	Coins	
Marsh Range	*c.* 1908	Coins	
Nelson Street	1966	Radiate copy of Victorinus	269–271
New Quay Road	1981	Denarius of Domitian	81–96
Quernmore Road	1979	Radiate of Postumus	260–268
	1981	AE of Domitian	81–96
Springfield Street	1950	Crispina	*c.* 180

(These coins are included in the Lancaster list).

B. A few coins have been recorded from areas around Lancaster.

Bolton-le-Sands	1988	Dupondius of Antoninus (*RIC* 803)	145–161
Borwick	1982	Sestertius of Trajan	103–117
Burrow Heights	1981	Radiate copy of Claudius II	268–270
Carnforth	?	Radiate of Postumus	259–268
Caton (Artlebeck Bridge)	*c.* 1940	3 Imperial AE Coins of Alexandria	
(One each of Hadrian and Antoninus; one illegible)			
Caton (Old Hall Farm)	1979	Radiate	*c.* 235–260
Docker Moor	1975	Hoard of 123 Radiates (see p. 68)	
Dolphinholme	1974	AE of Helena (*LRBC* I.1416)	326–330
Ellel	?	AE of Constans (*LRBC* I. 1142)	337–341
Halton-on-Lune	1979	2 AE Coins	1st/2nd C
Hornby Castle	19th C.	A number of coins, including Antoninus Pius (Watkin 1883, 218)	
Heysham	1903	Faustina I	138+
	1960	AE of Constantius II	
Morecambe	1979	AE of Arcadius (*LRBC* II.2436)	395–408
Silverdale	*c.* 1950	AE of Maximian (*RIC* (Ticinum) 29b)	294–300
Silverdale	1970	2 Denarii of Alexander Severus and Julia Mamaea (see p. 68)	222–235
Silverdale	1985	Sestertius of Trajan	103–117

Silverdale	1985	AE of Constantine I (*LRBC* I.59) (2 specimens)	331
Tunstall	1985	Sestertius of Septimius Severus (*RIC* 652)	193

ABBREVIATIONS

Arch. Journ.:	Archaeological Journal
BAR:	British Archaeological Reports
CIL:	Corpus Inscriptionum Latinarum
Crawford:	Crawford M. H., Roman Republican Coinage, Cambridge 1974
CW²:	Transactions of the Cumberland and Westmorland Antiquarian and Archaeological Society: Second series
Hill:	Hill P. V., *The Coinage of Septimius Severus and his Family of the Mint of Rome*, London 1977
HSLC:	Transactions of the Historic Society of Lancashire and Cheshire
JRS:	Journal of Roman Studies
LAAA:	Liverpool Annals of Anthropology and Archaeology
Lancs. Arch. Journ.:	Lancashire Archaeological Journal
LCAS:	Transactions of the Lancashire and Cheshire Antiquarian Society
LRBC:	Hill P. V., Carson R. A. G. and Kent J. P. C., *Late Roman Bronze Coinage*, London 1960
PPS:	Proceedings of the Prehistoric Society
PSAS:	Proceedings of the Society of Antiquaries of Scotland
RIB:	Collingwood R. G. and Wright R. P., *The Roman Inscriptions of Britain*, Oxford 1965
RIC:	Mattingly H., Sydenham E. A. and Sutherland C. H. V. (Edd)., *The Roman Imperial Coinage*, London 1923–83

BIBLIOGRAPHY

Anon 1865	Anon, *Leaves from Local History*
Anon 1908	Anon, *Catalogue of the Old Lancaster Exhibition*
Baines 1825	Baines E., *History, Directory and Gazetteer of the County Palatine of Lancaster*, Liverpool
Bellis and Penney 1979–80	Bellis R. and Penny S., The Lancaster *Vicus*: Excavation in Church Street, 1978, *Contrebis* VII, 4–31.
Birley 1936	Birley E. B., A Roman Altar from Bankshead; CIL VII. 802, *CW²* XXXVI, 1–7
Birley 1939	Birley E. B., The Beaumont Inscription, The Notitia Dignitatum, and the Garrison of Hadrian's Wall, *CW²* XXXIX, 190–226.
Birley 1947	Birley E. B., The Roman Fort at Low Borrow Bridge, *CW²* XLVII, 1–19
Brownbill 1915	Brownbill J., (ed), The Coucher Book of Furness Abbey, IIpt.1, Chetham Soc., LXXIV, 184 ff
Camden 1610	Camden W., *Britannia*, London
Casey 1978	Casey P. J., A Further Component of the Beaumont Hoard, 1855, *Coin Hoards* IV, 50–55
Casey and Reece 1974	Casey P. J. and Reece R., (Edd), *Coins and the Archaeologist*, BAR 4, Oxford
Chandler 1982	Chandler C., Excavations at Fairfield Road/West Road, Lancaster, *Contrebis* IX, 11–14
Clark 1807	Clark C., *An Historical and Descriptive Account of the Town of Lancaster*, Lancaster.
Cox 1720	Cox Thomas, *Magna Britannia*, London
Crawford 1974	Crawford M. H., *Roman Republican Coinage*, Cambridge
Cross Fleury 1891	Cross Fleury (Rigby R. E. K.), *Time-Honoured Lancaster: Historic Notes on the Ancient Borough of Lancaster*, Lancaster
Davies 1971	Davies R. W., The Roman Military Diet, *Britannia* II, 122–42
Docton 1957	Docton K. H., 'Lancaster 1684', *HSLC* CIX, 125–42
Edwards 1969	Edwards B. J. N., Lancashire Archaeological Notes: Prehistoric and Roman. *HSLC* CXXI, 99–108

Edwards 1971	Edwards B. J. N., Roman Finds from,'Contrebis', *CW²* LXXI, 17–33
Edwards 1988	Edwards B. J. N., The Wery Wall, pp. 21–23 in Jones G. D. B. and Shotter D. C. A. *Roman Lancaster*, Manchester
Edwards and Webster 1985	Edwards B. J. N. and Webster P. V., (Edd), *Ribchester Excavations, Part I*, Cardiff
Ellis 1986–7	Ellis M., A Roman Cremation Burial from Lancaster, *Contrebis* XIII, 32
Ellis 1987	Ellis M., 80 Church Street, Lancaster, 1985, *Contrebis* XIV, 18–19
Fowler 1975	Fowler P. J. (Ed), *Recent work on Rural Archaeology*, Bradford-upon-Avon
Goodburn and Bartholomew 1976	Goodburn R. and Bartholomew P., (Edd), *Aspects of the Notitia Dignitatum*, BAR 15, Oxford
Gregson 1869	Gregson M., *Portfolio of fragments relative to the History and Antiquities of the County Palatine and Duchy of Lancaster*. Third Edition, London
Grimes 1930	Grimes W. F., Holt, Denbighshire. The Works-Depot of the Twentieth Legion at Castle Lyons, *Y Cymmrodor* XLI
Hanson 1988	Hanson W. S., The Timber-lined well, pp. 179–183 in Jones G. D. B. and Shotter D. C. A., *Roman Lancaster*, Manchester
Harker 1878	Harker J., *British Interments on Lancaster Moor*, Lancaster
Hartley 1972	Hartley B. R., The Roman Occupations of Scotland: the evidence of Samian Ware, *Britannia* III. 1–55
Hassall 1976	Hassall M. W. C., Britain in the Notitia, pp. 103–117 in Goodburn R. and Bartholomew P. (Edd), *Aspects of the Notitia Dignitatum*, BAR 15, Oxford
Higham 1979a	Higham N. J. (Ed), *The Changing Past*, Manchester
Higham 1979b	Higham N. J., An Aerial Survey of the Upper Lune Valley, pp.31–38 in Higham N. J. (Ed), *The Changing Past*, Manchester
Higham 1980	Higham N. J., Native Settlements west of the Pennines, pp.41–47 in Branigan K. (Ed), *Rome and the Brigantes*, Sheffield
Higham and Jones 1975	Higham N. J. and Jones G. D. B., Frontier, Forts and Farmers, *Arch. Journ.* CXXXII, 16–53
Higham and Jones 1985	Higham N. J. and Jones G. D. B., *The Carvetii*, Gloucester
Hill 1977	Hill P. V., *The Coinage of Septimius Severus and his family of the mint of Rome*, London
Hinchcliffe and Williams f/c	Hinchcliffe J. and Williams J. H., *Roman Warrington: Excavations at Wilderspool 1966–9 and 1976*, Manchester
Hind 1974	Hind J. G. F., The Roman Name for Manchester, pp. 159–163 in Jones G. D. B. and Grealey S., *Roman Manchester*, Altrincham

Hogg 1965 | Hogg R., Excavation of the Roman auxiliary tilery, Brampton. *CW²* LXV, 133–168

Howard-Davis 1983–4 | Howard-Davis C., Lancashire Sites and Monuments Record and its Computerization, *Contrebis* XI, 3–25

Jarrett 1976 | Jarrett M. G., *Maryport, Cumbria: a Roman Fort and its Garrison*, Kendal

Johnson 1907 | Johnson A., On the Gallo-Roman Potters' marks on Terra Sigillata (Samian) Ware, found at Lancaster and Quernmore, *LCAS* XXIV, 5–6

Johnson 1909 | Johnson A., Supplementary List of Roman Potters' marks found at Lancaster, *LCAS* XXVI, 111

Jones 1968 | Jones G. D. B., The Romans in the Northwest, *Northern History* III, 1–26

Jones 1975 | Jones G. D. B., The North-western Interface pp. 93–106 in Fowler P. J. (Ed), *Recent Work on Rural Archaeology*, Bradford-Upon-Avon

Jones 1979 | Jones G. D. B., Archaeology and Coastal Change in the North-west. pp. 87–102 in Thompson F. H. (Ed), *Archaeology and Coastal Change*, London

Jones 1982 | Jones G. D. B., The Solway Frontier: Interim Report, 1976–81, *Britannia* XIII, 283–297

Jones and Grealey 1974 | Jones G. D. B. and Grealey S., *Roman Manchester*, Altrincham

Jones and Shotter 1988 | Jones G. D. B. and Shotter D. C. A., *Roman Lancaster*, Manchester

Jones M. 1975 | Jones M. J., *Roman Fort Defences to AD 117*, BAR 21, Oxford

King 1970 | King A., *Early Pennine Settlement: A Field Study*, Clapham

Leather 1972 | Leather G. M., *Roman Lancaster: Some Excavation Reports and some Observations*, Preston

Leather and Webster 1988 | Leather G. M. and Webster P. V., The Quernmore Kilns, pp. 85–93 in Jones G. D. B. and Shotter D. C. A., *Roman Lancaster*, Manchester

Leigh 1700 | Leigh R., *The Natural History of Lancashire*, Oxford

Lewis 1966 | Lewis M. J. T., *Temples in Roman Britain*, Cambridge

Lort 1779 | Lort M., Antiquities discovered in Lancaster, 1776, *Archaeologia* V, 98–100

Lowndes 1963 | Lowndes R. A. C., 'Celtic' Fields, farms and burial mounds in the Lune Valley, *CW²* LXIII, 77–95

Lowndes 1964 | Lowndes R. A. C., Excavation of a Romano–British Farmstead at Eller Beck, *CW²* LXIV, 1–14

Lukis 1883 | Lukis W. C. (Ed.), *Stukeley's Diaries and Letters*, 2, Surtees Soc. Vol. LXXVI, 240–1 and 245

Manning 1975	Manning W. H., Economic influences on land use in the military areas of the Highland Zone during the Roman period, pp. 112–116 in Evans J. G., Limbrey S. and Cleere H. (Eds.), *The Effect of Man on the Landscape: the Highland Zone*, CBA Research Report no. 11
Mayer 1852	Mayer J., *Catalogue of the Egyptian Museum, no.VIII, Colquitt Street, Liverpool*, Liverpool
Oldfield and Statham 1964–5	Oldfield F., and Statham D. C., Stratigraphy and Pollen Analysis on Cockerham and Pilling Mosses, North Lancashire, *Manchester Memoirs* CVII, no. 6, 1–16
Olivier 1987a	Olivier A. C. H., The Nature of the Ribchester Civil Settlement, pp. 117–126 in Edwards B. J. N. and Webster P. V. (Eds.), *Ribchester Excavations, Part 2*, Cardiff
Olivier 1987b	Olivier A. C. H., Excavation of a Bronze Age Funerary Cairn at Manor Farm, near Borwick, North Lancashire, *PPS* LII, 129–186
Pennant 1776	Pennant T., *A Tour in Scotland and Voyage to the Hebrides*, London
Penney 1975	Penney S. H., Gazetteer, *Contrebis* III, 2, 92
Penney 1977	Penney S. H., Excavations at Castle Park, Lancaster, *Contrebis* V, 40
Penney 1981	Penney S. H., *Lancaster, The Evolution of its townscape to 1800*, Lancaster, Centre for North-west Regional Studies
Penney 1982	Penney S. H., Excavation at no. 41, Church Street, Lancaster, *Contrebis* IX, 1–10
Penney 1983	Penney S. H., Romano-British Iron Extraction in North Lancashire, CW^2 LXXXIII, 59–61
Potter 1979	Potter T. W., *The Romans in North-West England*, Kendal
Reece 1974	Reece R., Numerical Aspects of Roman Coin Hoards in Britain, pp. 78–94 in Casey P. J. and Reece R. (Eds.), *Coins and the Archaeologist*, BAR 4, Oxford
Richmond 1936	Richmond I. A., Roman Leaden Sealings from Brough-under-Stainmore, CW^2 XXXVI, 104–125
Richmond 1938	Richmond I. A., The Roman Fort at Bewcastle, CW^2 XXXVIII, 195–237
Richmond 1950	Richmond I. A., Excavations at the Roman Fort of Newstead, 1947, *PSAS* LXXXIV, 1–37
Richmond 1954	Richmond I. A., Queen Cartimandua, *JRS* XLIV, 43–52
Richmond 1959	Richmond I. A., in *JRS* XLIX, 106–8
Richmond and Crawford 1949	Richmond I. A. and Crawford O. G. S., The British Section of the Ravenna Cosmography, *Archaeologia* XCII, 1–50
Rivet 1970	Rivet A. L. F., The British Section of the Antonine Itinerary, *Britannia* I, 34–82

Rivet and Smith 1979	Rivet A. L. F., and Smith C., *The Place-Names of Roman Britain*. London.
Robertson 1974	Robertson A. S., Romano-British Coin-Hoards: their numismatic archaeological and historical significance, pp. 12–26 in Casey P. J. and Reece R. (Eds.), *Coins and the Archaeologist*, BAR 4, Oxford
Rodwell 1975	Rodwell W., Milestones, Civic Territories and the Antonine Itinerary, *Britannia* VI, 76–101
Shotter 1972	Shotter D. C. A., Silver Denarii from Silverdale, Lancashire, *CW²* LXXII, 333–4
Shotter 1973a	Shotter D. C. A., *Numeri Barcariorum*: A Note on *RIB* 601, *Britannia* IV, 206–209
Shotter 1973b	Shotter D. C. A., *Romans in Lancashire*, Clapham
Shotter 1978a	Shotter D. C. A., Roman Coin Hoards in Lancashire, *Lancs. Arch. Journ.* I, 9–46
Shotter 1978b	Shotter D. C. A., Three Early Imperial Hoards from Lancashire, *Coin Hoards* IV, 44–5
Shotter 1979a	Shotter D. C. A., Watercrook and Ravenglass: the names and the garrisons, pp. 315–320 in Potter T. W., *The Romans in North-West England*, Kendal
Shotter 1979b	Shotter D. C. A., Coin Evidence and the Roman occupation of North-West England, pp. 1–13 in Highham N. J., *The Changing Past*, Manchester
Shotter 1982	Shotter D. C. A., The Roman Coin Hoard from Docker Moor, *CW²* LXXXII, 198–9
Shotter 1983	Shotter D. C. A., A Note on Tiles found on the Mitre Yard, Lancaster, in 1973, *Britannia* XIV, 270–1
Shotter 1984	Shotter D. C. A., *Roman North-West England*, Lancaster, Centre for North-West Regional Studies
Shotter 1985	Shotter D. C. A., The Coinage of Roman Ribchester: a Discussion, pp. 86–93 in Edwards B. J. N. and Webster P. V. (Eds.), *Ribchester Excavations, Part I*, Cardiff
Shotter 1986	Shotter D. C. A., A Roman Hoard from Cliburn, Penrith, *CW²* LXXXVI, 250–5
Shotter and James 1984	Shotter D. C. A. and James A., Roman Coin Hoard(s) from Hainings Farm, Kirksteads, Carlisle, *CW²* LXXIV, 260–2
Simpson 1852	Simpson R., *The History and Antiquities of the Town of Lancaster*, Lancaster
Stukeley 1776	Stukeley W., *Itinerarium Curiosum*, London
Thompson 1979	Thompson F. H. (Ed.), *Archaeology and Coastal Change*, London
Toulmin Smith	Smith L. Toulmin (Ed.), *Leland's Itinerary* IV, 11, London 1910

Watkin 1883   Watkin W. T., *Roman Lancashire*, Liverpool

Watson 1986–7   Watson W. G., Excavations at Cheapside, Lancaster, 1984, *Contrebis* XIII, 18–19

Webster 1969   Webster G., *The Roman Imperial Army*, London

West 1778   West T., *A Guide to the Lakes*, Kendal

White 1974   White A. J., Excavations in the *Vicus*, Lancaster 1973–4, *Contrebis* II, 2, 16–20

White 1975   White A. J., Excavations at No. 1 Penny Street, Lancaster, 1975, *Contrebis* III, 1, 30–3

White 1987   White A. J., *Roman Lancaster*, Lancaster City Museums, Local Studies No. 4, Lancaster

Wilson 1988   Wilson D. G., Horsedung from Roman Lancaster: a Botanical Report, pp. 170–178 in Jones G. D. B. and Shotter D. C. A., *Roman Lancaster*, Manchester